There's
No
Elevator
to the
Top

There's No Elevator to the Top

A Leading Headhunter Shares
the Advancement Strategies of the
World's Most Successful
Executives

Umesh Ramakrishnan

PORTFOLIO

PORTFOLIO
Published by the Penguin Group
Penguin Group (USA) Inc., 375 Hudson Street, New York, New York 10014, U.S.A. • Penguin Group (Canada), 90 Eglinton Avenue East, Suite 700, Toronto, Ontario, Canada M4P 2Y3 (a division of Pearson Penguin Canada Inc.) • Penguin Books Ltd, 80 Strand, London WC2R 0RL, England • Penguin Ireland, 25 St. Stephen's Green, Dublin 2, Ireland (a division of Penguin Books Ltd) • Penguin Books Australia Ltd, 250 Camberwell Road, Camberwell, Victoria 3124, Australia (a division of Pearson Australia Group Pty Ltd) • Penguin Books India Pvt Ltd, 11 Community Centre, Panchsheel Park, New Delhi–110 017, India • Penguin Group (NZ), 67 Apollo Drive, Rosedale, North Shore 0632, New Zealand (a division of Pearson New Zealand Ltd) • Penguin Books (South Africa) (Pty) Ltd, 24 Sturdee Avenue, Rosebank, Johannesburg 2196, South Africa

Penguin Books Ltd, Registered Offices: 80 Strand, London WC2R 0RL, England

First published in 2008 by Portfolio, a member of Penguin Group (USA) Inc.

10 9 8 7 6 5 4 3 2 1

LIBRARY OF CONGRESS CATALOGING IN PUBLICATION DATA
Ramakrishnan, Umesh.
   There's no elevator to the top : a leading headhunter shares the advancement strategies of the world's most successful executives / Umesh Ramakrishnan.
      p. cm.
   Includes bibliographical references and index.
   ISBN 978-1-59184-225-5 (alk. paper)
   1. Executive ability. 2. Leadership. 3. Executives. 4. Career development. 5. Success in business.
I. Title.
   HD38.2 R35 2008
   658.4'09—dc22   2008024977

Printed in the United States of America
Designed by Chris Welch

To the man before me, my father, P. V. Ramakrishnan,

and

to the man after me, my son, Neel Ramakrishnan.

I continue to learn from both.

Contents

Introduction

've got the best job in the world. I meet and speak with CEOs every day. As vice-chairman of one of the leading executive search firms in the world, I'm in the enviable position of having my finger on the pulse of global leadership. You would think that after all these years, I'd be jaded and my enthusiasm to meet new leaders would have ebbed. Well, it hasn't.

As the world changes, so do its leaders. When the economy is doing well, you tend to meet leaders who are people-oriented, persuasive, and sensitive. When the economy dips, the leaders in greatest demand are those who are tough, exacting, and able to make the really difficult calls that can affect large numbers of people (like laying off thousands of workers). And while there are leadership traits that are common around the globe, leadership styles differ from continent to continent. In addition, different industries call for different strategic and tactical skills.

Often, when someone new finds his way into the corner office, it's because the shareholders of the company want change and they've decided the old leadership can't deliver that change. While aspiring C-suiters may think they are able to start with a clean slate, many are shocked by the existing deck of cards they have to play with: a deck that does not permit them to institute the change they know is needed immediately. You can only properly understand that by talking to someone who has experienced it.

As I interview up-and-coming executives around the globe, I sense a real thirst for understanding the "secrets of the C-suite," the realm of the corporate world's chief officers. The C-suite, for the uninitiated, is the current nomenclature for the offices that house the company's executive management—people with titles that begin with "Chief." No matter how stoic the leader, I often detect a lack of confidence, despite their success and the achievements needed to get that job. They don't know what they don't know and it unsettles them.

On the other hand, I found that successful executives who were already there were very open about their successes and failures. One of them put it to me so plainly that I had to go back in my mind to see whether I'd missed something: "Those who make it to really high levels may not even realize they are on the journey." Now, on behalf of those who are just setting out, perhaps not even aware that they've done so, I have been able to ask those who have made it to the top tier of their respective industries—and stayed there—the question that is at the heart of this book: What do you know now that you wished you had known twenty years ago?

For me personally, this book was a challenge, too. I still had my day job, and interviewing executives all over the world would mean more traveling and more pressure for a year. I called my boss, Brian Sullivan, chairman and CEO of CTPartners. I needed his approval as this would take a considerable amount of worldwide resources and time. It took him thirty seconds. "This is who we are," he said. "This is what we do. You have my personal support for this effort." And since that was the case, I asked him about the most interesting interview he had had with a client. He told me about the time he interviewed a successful CEO, "a Fulbright scholar, collegiate sports legend, and a highly decorated military officer. When I asked what his greatest accomplishment was, he responded, 'My grandchildren.'"

This was not the last time I was going to hear something as unexpected as this as I embarked on my search for the difference makers in top executives' careers. Indeed, Walt Bettinger, president and COO of the investment services firm Charles Schwab, told me quite simply: "The best leaders will be successful at life, not simply at work."

To make sure the book had an authentic global perspective, I traveled for months, interviewed dozens of leaders in Europe, Asia, and North and South America and asked them to demystify the corner office for executives who were working hard to get there. Although I've written the book, the words of advice come directly to you from these leaders. I'm as much the messenger as the medium. I found all of them gracious and accommodating. They were incredibly generous in sharing their hard-earned knowledge with the prospective leaders of the future.

There were many surprises along the way. At one stage I realized that just about every executive told me the same thing—that they got inspiration from "the receptionist at the front desk." They all seemed to say it the same way, too. Unlike those other things I knew "theoretically," this wasn't what I was expecting. I was expecting a childhood tale or something involving some great inspirational figure at a sensitive moment in their lives. "Yet you've all used the same words," I said to one of them. "You know—I was inspired by my janitor or by my driver."

Other pieces of advice struck a distinct chord. People reviewing the book prior to publication have told me that they wished they had read it twenty years ago. Their careers might have been different. But this book is not about killer insights and things no one had ever thought of. After all, management is a much-studied discipline. Another interesting piece of feedback was that although the executives interviewed for the book are from industries, the lessons are applicable to executives leading any organization from corporations to schools, hospitals, or any large establishment that employs people.

The key to the book can be found in its purpose: I set out to examine and dissect the management principles and insights that fill the pages of the best-selling business books of our day. In one exchange I asked a chief financial officer about what he described as "executive maturity." Of course, I said, I know it comes through experience. But I wanted to dig deeper. What were the key elements of experience that aspirant young leaders need to master? Every time I pushed, the answers came—not catchphrases or labels, not textbook chapter heads or PowerPoint boxes, but detailed insights steeped in personal knowledge and laced with real-life stories and examples, many of them poignant, many funny, most both of those things.

So we laughed a lot. Sometimes just reflecting on what one does can seem funny. Kenneth Hicks, chief merchandising officer at JCPenney, half-jokingly told me: "The problem with our job is we don't really do anything. I mean, people at our level—I mean, it's a terrible thing to say." Delighted at the thought of where this might be going, I replied: "No, I think it's a great thing to say." And then I got what I was looking for: "We don't *do* it. We provide the resources, the guidance, direction, for all the people underneath us, who work with us, and the only way we can do that is in meetings. Otherwise, you meet one person at a time, and you have a line of people outside the door." There it was: an amusing—and honest—picture of life at the top.

In a similar vein, veteran retailer Rick Dreiling explained what it felt like when he took over at Duane Reade, the largest drugstore chain in the New York City metropolitan area: "I got here the week before Thanksgiving," he said, "and you know how it is. I'm sure you've placed a lot of CEOs—they call you about two weeks later and go: 'Did you know what I know now?' Right? And I mean, I was here two weeks and all of a sudden you're going, *Oh my God.* . . . " He displayed mock dismay as he proceeded to tell me about the moment he realized just how much harder the job was going to be than he thought. It was that kind of fresh and frank humor that filled my days with delight interviewing people for this book.

I tried to talk to executives from a range of places, industries, and backgrounds. I interviewed leaders of Fortune 100 companies and CEOs of start-up corporations. I spoke with both men and women. The youngest was barely thirty, the oldest past sixty. One was a young female CEO running a construction company in the Middle East, a potpourri of ironies if ever there was one. Another was the brother of the prime minister of an Asian country who was a leader in his own right. I also met with an African American CEO who headed a world-renowned financial services firm and an executive who grew up in India, lived in the United States, and then led a French telecom giant in the United Kingdom.

Wildly divergent views? Not really. There is a common thread of leadership without which the world's great corporations would not be able to function. As Terrance Marks, president of Coca-Cola Enterprises, put it: "You know, it's funny, the more time you spend [doing this] or the older you get, you find out that the advice you have to impart is increasingly less original. There's probably a good reason for that." But very little of what I heard from any of them was pat, tired, or formulaic.

One executive with a background in the armed forces, Kenneth Hicks of JCPenney, gave this somewhat chilling piece of advice: "The military is actually a very good place to really learn leadership. People think, Well, in the military you just give them an order, right? And they just do it. And I said, Okay, think about this. You're making

$30,000 a year. Somebody comes up to you and says, 'I want you to get in that Humvee, I want you to drive down that road and do it because it's the right thing to do for the country.' 'But I could get killed doing that. And if I don't do it, what will you do? You'll send me back to the States?' 'Yeah.' 'So I can take a risk and go out and possibly get killed because I'm doing what you want me to do and I believe in you and the mission that we have—or I can go back home?'" As Hicks demonstrates, it is possible to make common people do uncommon things with the right leadership traits.

Where I found the most differences was in the core functional strengths of individuals from different industries. Leaders from the retail industry had merchandizing and marketing strengths. PC makers were very detail oriented as they had to work very hard to keep their firms profitable. Financial service industry executives were able to articulate broad strategic plans, and service industry CEOs, as you might expect, were extremely customer focused, while technology leaders were visionaries. That is not to say that executives from one industry did not share strengths with their counterparts from different industries; rather, it was that their core strengths differed.

This makes for some interesting analysis regarding the best career paths for executives in different industries. For instance, without exposure to supply-chain management and accurate sales forecasting, it is almost impossible to lead a low-margin computer manufacturer. While it is important to get exposure to a broad range of functions on your way up, some functions are going to be more important than others, depending upon your industry.

There were times when someone would say something that seemed to capture the central question of the entire book. These statements were simple, yet compelling and powerful. Take Jim Donald, whom I interviewed within weeks of his losing his CEO job at Starbucks. He has an extraordinarily successful career in retail, going back to when he was a bag boy in a supermarket at age sixteen. You might think he could have claimed that there was something almost predestined about his career, something he could see or sense right at the start. But no: "I don't think anybody wakes up and says, I want to be a CEO. . . . I think people aspire to take on larger roles, more responsibilities, and lead more people. I think by people liking what they do and wanting to take on greater responsibilities, that—and depending upon their success—that naturally directs them to . . . a bigger area of responsibility. I never woke up and said, 'Hey, you know what? I think I'll be a CEO.' It just happens."

One of the other central questions I had was, What was the difference between a great executive and a mediocre one? Schwab's Walt Bettinger put it like this: "I'm of the view that the difference between the two is very small. It's less that one makes ninety percent good decisions and the other makes ten percent good decisions. They probably make about fifty percent of each, but the difference is that the executives who excel tend to maybe more quickly recognize which fifty percent are which and have the humility to admit to the wrong fifty percent and do something . . . about it."

Brian Sullivan confirmed this from our side of the table. He first pointed out that the average tenure of a CEO is about five years. "There have been a lot of CEOs in place for over ten years; therefore a significant amount must get fired in their second year in order to make the average work." Sullivan also had an important message for executives about what to do when they get things wrong: "Most CEOs have failures every month. Today's wow idea can be tomorrow's failure. CEOs must be alert to the market, their competitors, and their clients or customers. All three will let you know when you've failed, hopefully in time to correct it. Anyone who tells you they have had a failure-free career has committed one of the biggest failures—lack of self-awareness."

Another thing that may surprise people who have not spent a lot of time with top executives is that they are not always visibly charismatic. They all have what might be called executive presence, but not all of them inspire you with it. However, once you have spent significant time with them, you find that they are all inspirational in their own way.

I met with them in various places—at their offices, in restaurants, at conferences, and in airports. Not one of them seemed rushed. They seemed truly interested in people, and they knew I was working on a book aimed at people who wanted to know about them and what they did. As an executive recruiter who spends a lot of time with both established and wannabe executives, my "BS meter" is pretty good. While some of them hammed a little for the book, most were genuine, even with seemingly clichéd issues such as team building, communication, passion, and the like. The most repeated answer to the question "What were some of the things you found in the C-suite that you did not expect but which made you feel happy about being there?" was that they did not realize the extent of fulfillment they would gain from mentoring and nurturing potential successors.

One of the CEOs I met early in the process told me that the reason he had agreed to be interviewed for the book was that I was "going to the source." Although I have led companies, I did not want to stand on the sidelines of global corporations and espouse theory after theory as a consultant might. Those books lie like skeletons across the publishing graveyard. I wanted this to be a book by successful executives for ambitious managers whose primary career goal was to someday lead a corporation. I did not want to focus on work alone, but also to ask more personal questions as well, such as how they managed to keep their marriages intact as they flitted across the globe seven days a week. They were disarmingly honest about issues like that. And they didn't all say the same thing. While some said it was lonely at the top, a CEO of one of the world's top telecom companies completely dismissed that notion and said that it was only as lonely as you made it out to be. He said that the key to keeping loneliness at bay had to do with one's circle of friends outside of work—keeping them the same before and after getting to the top and not treating them differently.

Over the years, I've observed a noticeable increase in the complexity that top executives have to deal with. With onerous regulatory laws such as Sarbanes-Oxley and increasingly activist shareholders, CEOs and those who report directly to them are probably under more pressure than ever. For many, there is only an unceremonious exit from the C-suite in their future, either because they've grown weary of the regulators or because they have not been able to adapt to rapidly changing conditions. I was struck by the number who said that the trip to the top may not be worth the hassle for everybody. One retiring CEO of one of the largest food products companies in the world told me that if the only ambition of a young employee is to become a CEO, then she is going to have a very difficult life because she will be constantly chasing an elusive goal and will not enjoy the more important part—the journey. There are many roads to success in the corporate world, and not all of them lead to the top job. It is entirely possible to have a successful, rewarding career without becoming CEO. Obviously, it is better to know this before you embark on that journey.

That's why I didn't hesitate to ask questions about life outside the office. I wanted to know if "work-life balance" was just management-speak to show your employees that you have a softer side. I found that although many of these leaders struggled with finding that balance, they would have done things differently if they had known how their personal lives would turn out. Without exception, they told me that without the support and understanding of their partner or spouse, they would be doomed to misery during those times when they are truly alone. And it isn't only understanding in the broad sense of the word, but an understanding of the extent of the effort that will be required to make it to the top and stay there.

They also unanimously cautioned managers about changing their colors and beliefs to suit the office politics of the day. That's a prescription for failure, since there will come a day in which that individual looks in the mirror and discovers that he or she has lost a sense of self. While these may feel like touchy-feely topics, the executives I spoke to advised others to think about such things long and hard before starting on their climb up the greasy pole.

Writing this book felt a bit like completing an MBA in an exclusive business school. Rather than listening to lectures, I heard them from successful leaders of today who have already reached the top. These were successful, driven individuals who got there by different means and in different circumstances. But they share certain common characteristics. Some of those characteristics are worn on their sleeves. Others are deep inside the individual, bubbling to the surface when the occasion demands it. As I dug deeper, I found the answers to the most fundamental questions, such as what made these leaders tick. Their responses made my interviews both exhilarating and inspiring. They impart an education that is not theoretical but based on that most credible qualification of a true teacher—proven success.

Through my work, I've also met with thousands of up-and-coming executives. Although I focus on top-level talent, ironically, it is the interaction with younger executives who have an eye on the corner office that led me to write this book. Here, too, I have found common characteristics, but these findings have been more alarming than inspiring. The one positive attribute that they do share with successful executives is ambition. However, ambition is only a catalyst and not the active ingredient in the formula for success. It needs to be mixed in equal measure with other essential elements such as a strong work ethic, innovation, creativity, survival, instincts, and adaptability. And although I can't remember more than one or two actually saying you need a sense of humor, almost everyone displayed ample talent in that department.

The overriding theme gleaned from the dozens of executives I spoke with is that there is no one express elevator to the top. In fact, several told me that you should avoid a speedy rise, as the faster you rise the quicker you fall. In the following pages, I hope you learn the same valuable lessons that I learned while writing this book. Some may not seem new, but have been lost over time, settling to the bottom of the collective consciousness of an overconfident society. And I hope you have as much fun reading it as I had writing it.

Chapter 1

First Steps

Steve Reinemund had no grand plan to become a CEO. "When I talk to students on college campuses, all they really want to know is, What is the roadmap to becoming a CEO? There isn't one. At least if there is one, I don't have it," he admitted to me when we met at his office in Dallas. "Many of us who became CEOs didn't start out with that objective. We just sort of got there. If you enjoy your journey, and you're good at it, you'll get more opportunities, and if you're lucky, you just might become CEO."

Reinemund, who was just entering his sixties when we sat down together, makes his career trajectory sound serendipitous. That is counterintuitive, considering his impressive twenty-two-year tenure at PepsiCo, the last five as CEO (he retired in May 2007). A graduate of the U.S. Naval Academy, he served five years as an officer in the United States Marine Corps and achieved the rank of captain. He even had a few stints guarding the White House during parts of the Nixon and Ford administrations. He later earned an MBA at the University of Virginia before beginning an impressive career in business. As we go to press, Steve informed me of his appointment as the dean of business and professor of leadership and strategy at Wake Forest University. The students there are a lucky bunch.

Reinemund's sentiments are echoed by many of the CEOs of multibillion-dollar companies who shared their stories for this book. In fact, many attributed their success to the fact that they *didn't* fixate on visions of a big mahogany desk and a corner office. Instead they focused on their work, and the rewards followed.

Others thought the drive came from deep down inside, a "force" within you, not necessarily taking you to the top, but taking you to a point at which you settle for nothing less than excellence. Rick Dreiling of Duane Reade put it this way when I met him in a conference room just off his office in New York: "There's a burning desire, I think, in every CEO—and it isn't the burning desire to be a CEO. I think it's the burning desire to be the best you can be. . . . I mean, you hear all these stories about CEOs talk[ing] about how they did this when they were a kid and that when they were a kid. I think it's just a burning desire that I can do it, that I can do it better, and I want to drag a bunch of people along with me to do it." (Not long after our interview, Dreiling, now in his mid-fifties, was recruited to become CEO of Dollar General by Kohlberg Kravis Roberts & Co., which acquired the discount chain in 2007.)

That is not to say that you shouldn't plan a journey to the C-suite or that you shouldn't allow yourself to think about it, even early in your career. In fact, it's never too early to start thinking about it. But make sure you concentrate on doing the job at hand, building upon the skills and opportunities you have now. You'll be noticed and promoted—and will be that much more prepared as you take on increasing amounts of responsibility throughout your career.

Indeed, ambition is important, but, as Reinemund said, there's a difference between driving to achieve excellence in what you're doing and driving to achieve career development and advancement. "If you do the first one well, the second one will come," he said. "But if you focus entirely on the second one, it's likely you're not going to succeed at either."

Steve Shindler, chairman and CEO of NII (formerly Nextel International), which provides wireless and other mobile services to Latin American countries, had this to add to the conversation: "There are a million handbooks on how to be a CEO. Most of them are just opinions," he told me in his office in Virginia. "You're going to the source. You have to actually sit in this seat to feel the joy and the pain that goes with this job."

Follow Your Leaders

As Shindler suggests, go to the source—people who have lived and breathed the CEO experience. A lot can be learned by example. If you are among the fortunate few who had an experienced mentor early in life to help you with choices, you are already ahead of the game. But for most people, when you're young, it's difficult to ascertain the credibility of the advice that you receive. And while a lot of knowledge and understanding can come from study, nothing beats experience.

As you begin your career and move upward, take care to examine your supervisors. Are they the kind of leaders that inspire others to do better? Do they have integrity? Do they care enough about customer service? Some of them will turn out to serve as examples of what *not* to do—but that, too, is learning. Your good role models won't necessarily become your personal mentors, but that doesn't mean you can't learn from their examples.

"Look for people who have been successful at doing what you want to do and are willing to spend the time coaching you and giving you candid advice about what you could do to be more successful," John Swainson, CEO of CA, Inc., told me. "And what you really would like to have is someone who doesn't have an oar in the water. In other words, they're not directly affected by the outcome of your performance or your decision." Swainson, now in his mid-fifties, was able to put the lessons he learned from mentors to work when he took over at a troubled CA in February 2005, by immediately improving customer relations and expanding through acquisitions.

Bill Amelio is president and CEO of Lenovo, one of the world's largest makers of personal computers, which was formed by the Lenovo Group of China's acquisition of the former IBM Personal Computer Division. Amelio, who came to the company from Dell, began studying leaders' behavior well before the C-suite was in view, and he didn't just limit it to observing people in the corporate world. "When I was in college, I was fascinated by the ability of leaders from business to politics— to command attention, captivate people, and make them understand a vision," he recalled. He kept a close eye on what it was about those individuals that made them unique and then asked himself if he could do the same. "Suddenly I realized that leadership was in my blood and it became my passion." Amelio, the son of a Pittsburgh shoe repairman and now in his early fifties, started his career at IBM and then held positions with NCR and Honeywell. He has a master's in management from Stanford University and a bachelor's in chemical engineering from Lehigh University. It did not surprise me when Amelio told me he wanted to be in leadership positions. Manner and demeanor don't necessarily tell you about a person's leadership qualities, but Amelio looked to me like someone who knew and cared about what he was doing. He was dressed casually and spoke with considerable enthusiasm, driving home his points with expressive gestures. I felt charged up when I came out of our meeting at his offices in Singapore.

While clearly it's important to follow those who do well in their jobs, many of the executives I spoke with stressed that you should take note of how they handle setbacks—which can be a vital measure of true leadership. "Success is a lousy teacher," Rick Dreiling told me bluntly. "The more successful you tend to be, the more behind you can get." It was classic Dreiling, who has a way of energizing people while putting them at ease. As we headed to his office after he came to meet me, he greeted his employees with the manner of a friendly and wise college professor hailing his students and colleagues.

Lucas Chow, CEO of the Singapore-based media conglomerate MediaCorp Group, echoed Dreiling's warning about the perils of too much success. He told me over tea at the Raffles Hotel, "You can celebrate success for a short duration of time, but it is soon forgotten. But you benefit from mistakes for a lifetime." Chow, now in his mid-fifties, joined MediaCorp as its group CEO in 2005 from Sing-Tel. Before that he spent twenty years at Hewlett-Packard.

Bob Reynolds, vice-chairman and chief operating officer of privately owned Fidelity Investments, the largest mutual-fund company in the United States, made a little joke out of the question of mistakes, and in the process secured the idea in my mind. I had asked him a question that I had put to all my interviewees: "Any mistakes that people can learn from?" He said there were "probably a lot but I don't focus on them." He's a positive kind of guy. "Yeah. I'm not a negative guy. . . . This sounds funny but, you know, the best way to build up customer loyalty is to make a mistake and fix it." A colleague present during the interview interjected: "Not that you strive for that but you're right." Reynolds couldn't resist it: "Yeah. Well, you know, one time we talked [about] . . . 'Okay, how do we make a mistake?'" He was joking, of course, but was making a valid point at the same time. Every executive should strive to continually improve the company's products or services from a customer perspective. Customers reward this perseverance with loyalty.

Probably one of the most challenging routes to the top is being seen as a potential successor to a legendary figure. Walt Bettinger at

Charles Schwab has long been considered the most likely successor to Charles Schwab, founder and CEO, who is now in his seventies. I asked Bettinger what aspirant leaders need to know if they ever find themselves in that position.

Bettinger didn't try to dodge the question with any false modesty: "It's a fascinating topic," he said immediately. "When you serve an icon, as I have said many times, there's only room for one icon. And if someone aspires to be an icon themselves, they shouldn't be in an organization that is led by an icon. There is only one irreplaceable person at Charles Schwab, and that's Chuck and that's how it should be."

He added: "I must simply be Walt Bettinger. I am not Chuck Schwab and I will never be Chuck Schwab. And it would be a travesty to try to be Chuck Schwab."

Certainly Bettinger has no pretensions. His office in Cleveland (he maintains another office in San Francisco) is simply decorated, and evokes a quintessentially friendly midwestern atmosphere. A row of baseball bobblehead dolls caught my eye. And Bettinger, dressed casually, related warmly to those around him, chatting pleasantly with a member of his administrative staff about her upcoming vacation. It was easy to see why the employees of Charles Schwab would follow this leader.

Find Your Niche, But Don't Get Stuck in It

When I met Ron Williams, CEO of the healthcare giant Aetna, in his office in Hartford, the first thing he said he would advise aspiring C-suiters to do is zero in on exactly where in the business they want to be. "One of the most important decisions you can make is a sector call," he said. "Because businesses or sectors or industries have life cycles."

From a professional standpoint, the sooner you focus on where you want to fit in, the quicker you are likely to take off. This is not to say that you can't change your mind, but your superiors can sense focus and drive, and it comes across in people who are not wavering about where they want to be.

Once you've asked yourself if you prefer service versus operations, corporate versus retail, technology versus consulting, "look for opportunities that are problematic and challenging," Williams recommended. "People are much more interested in individuals who can add value and much less interested in what I call the 'central casting' phenomenon." The "central casting" phenomenon is something that we executive recruiters are also susceptible to. Sometimes, especially in sales-oriented roles, it is easy to be fooled by executives who articulate thoughts well, who have a commanding presence but little substance. This is usually discovered when they have to solve complex problems in their jobs. These "empty suits" tend to talk a lot but do not know how to implement a solution. It becomes readily apparent to those who follow whether the leader at the top is one who actually adds value and is key to solving the problem, or is someone who just waxes eloquent about potential solutions.

However, to Williams, the hallmark of a real leader is more prosaic—it is someone who can also look beyond his or her chosen sector. "I would say that the way you would recognize [leadership qualities] is when people no longer define every problem in the context of their functional specialty," Williams explained. "Meaning that if you come out of marketing, every problem you see is a marketing problem. Sometimes it's a human-resource problem. Sometimes it's a financial problem and sometimes it may be a technological problem. And so it's the ability to develop a broad enough perspective to properly categorize and frame business issues beyond your own functional expertise." It is important to recognize where you have been and the lens through which you have looked at problems. If you are shortsighted, then as a marketing executive, you are blind to the fact that the problem may have another dimension outside of your limited perspective, and you will not grow.

Eventually, when you've figured out what end of the building you want to be in and in what capacity you can fit, ask yourself what moves you. "There's a balance between finding something you're passionate about early and being willing to do the work required to build your skill base, which isn't always fun," Reinemund said. It helps an awful lot to love what you do, and if you don't, think hard about whether or not you should be doing something else.

Just about everyone I spoke to saw risk, and the willingness to take some risks, as a quality of an outstanding leader. No one suggested you should be reckless or foolhardy, but there is much to be said for the person who steps forward and says, "I'll try. Let me do it." Walt Bettinger of Charles Schwab said, "Go to your boss and say, 'Give me the dirtiest, nastiest, toughest problem you've got on your plate that has not been solved and let me have a crack at it.'" Ron Williams of Aetna said that one of the most gratifying functions of his job was to solve problems that could not be solved elsewhere. "If it was an obvious solution, it would have been solved somewhere else in the organization." Just as thinking outside of your specialization is an ability shared by true C-suiters, so is putting out fires when others can't.

At the very least, volunteering for the difficult jobs, and being prepared to take risks, will get you noticed. "I think most organizations will give up-and-coming young managers more credit than those who take easy businesses which are in an upswing anyway," Lee Hsien Yang, the former CEO of SingTel, told me. Take on overseas assignments or ask to be put on new ventures, and "you will definitely be recognized." Straightforward recognition was never a concern for Lee. He is the second son of Singapore's first prime minister, Lee

Kuan Yew, and brother of the current prime minister, Lee Hsien Loong. He also served in the armed forces, rising to the rank of brigadier general. But he knew what risk and recognition meant in the corporate world, and that was another matter. His name recognition would only go so far there, as clients around the world were largely ambivalent about his family connections but gave him credit or criticism based on his performance as a company leader. This was a concept that he was very comfortable with, and it seemed like he preferred it, as the bouquets and the brickbats that he received were solely of his own doing.

When I met with Sanjiv Ahuja, former CEO of the London-based mobile operator Orange, we talked at a small conference table in his office. The company's offices were liberally furnished with orange couches and sofas, creating a vibrant atmosphere. Ahuja himself, dressed in business-casual clothes, seemed to embody the new global executive—he grew up in India, worked in the United States, and is now the head of a French-owned company in London. "Leaders emerge out of crises, and people by nature perceive crises as risks," he said. "However, that's the time when the biggest opportunities are created. Leaders . . . step up at that time."

Risk sometimes means opting out. Arthur Collins, CEO of Medtronic, the medical technology company, warned about the dangers of not recognizing the fact that you are in a dead-end job, for example. "One of the most telling traces of a dead-end job is when you stop wondering about work challenges or when you stop being in a position where you are being stretched," he said. "You should always ask yourself if you are still as passionate about the job as the day you started. Passion drives energy and energy drives results. Without passion, a job becomes just a job and not a path to success." If you decide you are going to make a move, plot your next step carefully. Be honest about what skills you lack, develop a plan to fill those gaps, and then execute that plan with feedback from a coach or mentor.

Listen Carefully

Most corporations today have formal employee evaluation programs. A popular one is the "360-degree evaluation," where employees get active feedback on both performance and cultural fit from other employees above them, below them, and at their peer level. It is a holistic method of taking individual bias out of an evaluation. When Bill Amelio of Lenovo had his first 360-degree evaluation at Allied-Signal, it left an impression, to say the least. "I remember it like it was yesterday," he told me with a smile. "As I read the report, I was actually getting angry and marking up the report. Then, I suddenly 'got it.' A lightbulb went off. It was right there in black and white: I could either ignore the truth, or I could do something about it, change and become more effective," he said. "That was a major 'a-ha' moment for me . . . you have to be prepared and be willing to accept feedback. Now, when someone tells me something I really don't want to hear, I respond with gratitude. I say 'thank you,' and while I might not agree with the opinion, I consider it seriously and thoroughly. I really like people who have the courage to provide honest feedback. I value that tremendously."

Indeed, as he put it, "feedback is a gift." Many companies, like Lenovo, are incorporating 360-degree review programs to "get the good, the bad, and the ugly," as Amelio put it. Being willing not just to hear the bad, but to welcome the ugly, can be as big a test of your leadership aptitude as anything you are going to encounter before you get to the top. Make good use of it when it comes your way.

Carl Bass, president and CEO of Autodesk, a design technology company with headquarters in San Rafael, California, said his company has an executive coach who does extensive feedback. "And it's slightly less offensive than getting security clearance from the government," he quipped. "She goes and talks with your wife and your friends and your kids if they'll talk to her. . . . This woman went over and talked to my wife for four hours maybe. My kids at the time were four and five years old or something, so they didn't have a lot of insight."

Over about twelve to sixteen weeks, the interviews "with all the people involved in your life" are combined with a series of psychological and analytical tests designed to build a complete picture, he said. The coach observes you in staff meetings and "follows you around for a day or two . . . and interviews at least half a dozen to a dozen of your work colleagues." It was the most extensive 360 I'd ever heard of.

Bass was worried the review would be a painful experience. One of his colleagues described it to him as "like getting sunburned and having someone pull off the layers of skin one by one." But, Bass discovered, "It turns out it's not at all [painful] because the people we have to do this are very, very skillful. It certainly takes a unique personality to be able to do it."

When I asked Bill Amelio what aspiring C-suiters should do with feedback, he said, "They need to make sure they're listening carefully and they should also be able to look and say, Where are my skill gaps to be able to do that job? My desire someday is to do that job. What is it that I'm lacking right now that's keeping me from getting that job?"

John Kealey, CEO of iDirect Technologies, a privately held company that designs satellite-based broadband access solutions, also uses a 360-degree feedback system. And almost as important as the comments he gives to employees themselves are their reactions.

"One of the things I noticed was the people who scaled with our company as we grew were really open to what they were hearing in that feedback and were trying to make changes," he told me when we met in the start-up company's offices in Herndon, Virginia. "And some were afraid of it instead of owning it and dealing with it." That helped determine which people to keep in mind for upper-level jobs that opened up.

Listening is not just about feedback, however. It is also an often-neglected component of good executive communication. Not in the "tell me your troubles" kind of way, but in the way that acknowledges the expertise, the experience, and the genuine concerns of those people who do the job every day. "When I first came into this company," said Martin Homlish, who joined the business software solutions company SAP as global chief marketing officer, from Sony Corporation, "for the first six months, almost on a daily basis, I would set up informal lunch and breakfast meetings with a half-dozen employees from multiple areas around the company. The purpose was simply to say, 'Hi, guys. I'm here. I'm the new guy and I have two questions for you. First question, what's really working well? Tell me what's really working well and what you believe we should under no circumstances fix or change.'

" 'Then secondly, if we look at your role and how you can contribute to the overall strategy of the company, tell me one thing that's really not working well and how you think I can help you with that.' You'd be surprised. As simple as that—that very simple outreach." He truly believed that this simple step of reaching out and actually asking for their opinion and then helping them with the solution to their problem was an effective method of integrating himself with the team while at the same time establishing himself as a leader.

For the first two or three sessions, said Homlish, people were "quite leery . . . But after a week or so the word got out that (a) the new leader is listening, (b) it's not a test, and (c), most importantly, there were some actions that were taken quickly, addressing some of the things that needed to be fixed."

This is not about a comfortable, "steady-as-she-goes" approach. On the contrary, Homlish noted that "when you're working for a very successful company, it's sometimes difficult to help people embrace the idea that you should change while you are winning.

"If you're in a company such as mine, you have number-one market share, you have number-one market position, you've recorded double-digit growth for fifteen to twenty years in a row. Then you walk into that organization and you say, 'Oh, by the way, we need to change where we're going. We need to change what we're doing.' People will look at you and say, 'Gee, we're doing exceptionally well. Why do we need to change?'

"The answer is pretty simple. The best time to drive change is when you're winning. The best time to drive change is when you have positive momentum. The worst time to drive dynamic change is when you're losing because you don't have the market momentum, you don't have the people momentum."

There's a saying that you have two ears and one mouth and you should use them in that proportion. This is even more important when you get to the C-suite. However, all the benefits of listening are lost if you do not implement an action plan based on what you heard. Sometimes, that action plan is as simple as stating that you have evaluated all options and nothing has changed, but the mere fact that you address it lets your employees know that you've been listening.

When I asked Michael Dell what were some of the top characteristics he sought in an executive, this is what he had to say: "Great executives are great listeners first. Listen very carefully, ask a lot of questions, learn. I learned an early lesson in the value of getting a direct contact with the customer and not doing it in a random way, but doing it in a targeted manner. One of our core values here at Dell is 'curious'—we want them to be open to what they might discover through listening."

Never Stop Learning

There is no time to rest on your laurels on your way to the C-suite. This book is filled with insider tips and firsthand tales of what it's like to navigate through your career, but the CEOs I've spoken to also rely on the same tools you have at your bookstore or local university: old-fashioned book learning. Always strive to improve your skills and broaden your knowledge, even as you ascend the ladder and get closer to your goal. Ron Williams of Aetna, who has a BA in clinical psychology from Roosevelt University and an MS in management from the Sloan School, MIT, advocates visiting the business section at the bookstore as a way to stay current and deepen your understanding of the corporate world. "Books provide a way to fill in gaps, a way to stay current and develop a perspective that you wouldn't normally come into," he told me. "I also encourage people to take workshops, seminars, get out of their own foxhole, talk to other executives in similar or different industries."

Rick Dreiling said he thought it was important to keep abreast of what is going on in the world, and that means not just reading books, but periodicals as well: "I think that as a CEO it is very important that you . . . read magazines and newspapers and books. Some CEOs will tell you that 'that's why I have people and if there's anything important out there, they will bring it to me. They'll bring me the article.' I don't agree with that. I believe that my charge should be to walk into this room and say, 'Hey, I just read this article in *The Economist*, what do you all think about that?' or 'Here's something I saw in *Busi-nessWeek.*' "

And then there is the question of whether you need an MBA. Many of the executives I spoke to agreed that an MBA is not always required. "Go as far as you can go with your formal education, and as far as you want to go, and get it out of the way as early as you possibly can," Terrance Marks of Coca-Cola told me. Once you get going in the workforce, chances are you'll be moved around, perhaps be married with children, and won't have the flexibility to go to school. He did have a counterpoint on getting a graduate degree after beginning a career. "But you get so much more out of your education having been in the workforce, and have so much more context for what you're learning," Marks said. However, he concluded that "an MBA is nice to have, but it's not a need-to-have."

Lee Hsien Yang of SingTel agreed. "If you're doing really well, and you're reasonably confident, why do you want to do it?" he asked rhetorically. "It's a very expensive degree and is two years in opportunity costs." He continued by saying that if you want to change career directions—for example, move from functional to general management, or if you want a complete career shift—then an MBA is the way to go. "But if all you want to do is stay in the same company and you're doing well, why do you need it?" Lee himself has a first-class honors degree in engineering from Cambridge University and an MSc in management science from Stanford University.

But even if you've got that MBA, be careful that you don't drift into complacency about other forms of learning. "Just because you come into an environment and you have the piece of paper that says MBA, don't assume that you're smarter than many of the people that you will be working with who have another piece of paper which says ten, fifteen, twenty years of experience," said Martin Homlish of SAP. "Be willing to listen and learn and most importantly, you will actually learn the most from the people who are on the street and in the trenches doing the job and getting the work done." Homlish has a bachelor of arts degree in communications from Goddard College and continued his education at Babson College and the Columbia University Graduate School of Business. It is important to note that the requirements for an advanced degree differ from industry to industry. In a strategy-consulting organization, it is almost a requirement. Many of our clients prefer an advanced degree, but I can't remember a single one refusing to hire an accomplished executive simply based on the absence of one.

Steven Crane, chief financial officer of CMGI, the global provider of supply-chain services, felt it was important "not to give up" on your technical expertise. "Get out there and constantly train yourself . . . not necessarily through a school, but even just a technical-type conference. Stay on top of what you're doing," he urged. Crane has a master's in international management from the Thunderbird School of Global Management in Glendale, Arizona, and a BS in mechanical engineering from Tulane University in New Orleans.

Probably the most interesting story I heard about a senior executive continuing to learn came from Lucas Chow, CEO of MediaCorp. Chow said he had been trying to sell some of his company's telecom services to the hotel business. According to Chow, the general manager of the Raffles Hotel, one of Singapore's historic institutions, told him: " 'Hey, you know, instead of just coming to sell to the hotel, what value can you add?' So I told the CEO of this hotel, 'Look, the only way that I can add value to you is [by learning] your business, because I never worked one day in a hotel.' So she said, 'How would you learn that?' 'Let me work one day in your hotel and I guarantee you, I'll be able to give you some ideas.' And she did. She allowed me to work one day in the hotel. So early in the morning I came here and reported to work, from housekeeping all the way to the banquet and kitchen. I've seen all the booking and everything. I've seen the entire process."

Chow said he drew a comparison between the hotel business and hospitals, a sector that was very familiar to him. "There are four phases—the booking before you check in, the check-in itself, the stay-in experience, and the checkout experience. Customer satisfaction is drawn from exactly these four phases. Hotels and hospitals are the same. You know, hotels track the number of rooms and beds, extra beds. And hospitals track the same. Now knowing a bit of the technology I say, Why don't you do RFID (radio-frequency identification—electronic tagging of items), because with RFID instead of sending people up and down the whole building, in the whole hospital, to try to find empty beds and things like that, you will be able to tell instantly how many beds are located where, how many empty beds you have. If a guest wants an extra bed, you know exactly where to find it."

The lesson from this, said Chow, is that "inspiration comes when you have knowledge about a situation."

Health and Your Personal Life Matter

When I met Bob Reynolds of Fidelity in Boston, it was late summer and he had just returned from a fly-fishing trip in Jackson Hole. Now in his mid-fifties, he looked radiant and well rested. He even had a scraggly beard to show for his outdoor adventure. "I have never had a reaction like this," joked Reynolds. "I mean, I get calls from Pasadena, California. Yesterday a guy called from Washington, D.C., 'Hey, I hear you have a beard.' I'm like, 'What the hell's the big deal?' " The answer seemed to be, as Reynolds put it, that he had "never gone longer than three days without shaving—I didn't even know I could grow a beard."

Reynolds makes time to look after his mental and physical health. It helps that early on, he was a referee at the highest level in NCAA football. He loves golf, skiing, fishing for blues and bass, and collecting autographed baseballs.

At the early stages of your career you may not think about your health as a prerequisite for success, but you better believe it. Almost every executive I met was fit and healthy. Success won't be achieved by forgoing a morning run or evening workout just to stay in the office. Right from the start, you also have to develop physical strength and stamina.

François Barrault, CEO of BT Global Services, likens his job to training for a sports competition. When he steps off a transcontinental flight, instead of crashing out at the hotel, he puts on his running shoes. "The other day I went to Australia—a twenty-seven-hour total trip. Most people get rest and go to bed, but I went for a run and a swim for two hours." Barrault anticipates his busy seasons, when he'll be on the road more than at other times of the year, speaking with shareholders and clients, and he plans his regimen accordingly. "You have the season and the off-season," he said. "If you want to be successful when you speak in front of thousands of people, you need to come prepared as an [athlete]." To Barrault, who is in his mid-forties, that is what sets a leader apart.

Just as crucial as health and fitness, family is an essential part of your personal foundation that will help support you throughout your career. While all the executives I spoke to stressed the importance of a strong family life, they recognized that each person learns how to make it work for himself. Start by learning to negotiate with your family.

"If you don't have a strong relationship and the right agreement with your partner or spouse, you will not be successful," John Swainson of CA, Inc. told me. "You can't be, because you can't have the emotional stability."

Swainson also stressed how important it is to be honest about how you've set up your personal life to complement your high career goals. "The worst thing is people who are not honest with themselves about these personal choices and end up trying to do things that either they can't do or that their circumstances won't allow them to do," he said. "And then they become fundamentally unhappy because of the conflict that it creates. And you can't do these jobs if there's a fundamental conflict in your life." Chapter 7 is devoted to work-life balance, because it is vitally important to your chances of success.

Let Your Passion Guide You

Lucas Chow of MediaCorp wasn't afraid to wax sentimental on the subject of why you do your job and want to get to the top. For Chow, it's not the prestige, money, respect, or fame that a corner office might bring. Instead, he said, it's what is in his heart—and he encourages future C-suiters to ask themselves what really motivates them, what they are passionate about. It is this drive that Chow says is a characteristic he's seen in many managers whose paths he has crossed. "Successful managers I have worked with all share a common characteristic: passion," he said. "Ask successful managers how they find all their energy. It's passion. If you feel passionate about something, you will not get burned-out and you will not get tired about doing it, because you are passionate about it."

But just as Chow recommended letting your true passion lead you, it's also important to recognize when your passion dies. "The moment that you find yourself losing that passion, I think you should reevaluate your current position and your job," Chow warned. "It's almost like a person falling in love. How can you tell the person not to love? The person cannot sleep, cannot eat, cannot drink whole days long thinking about the other party. But the moment that passion is gone, relationships break down. So, to me, I think that without passion it's going to be very difficult." While some of the tools and skills you'll take with you to the C-suite can be learned, passion is something you need to possess from the start.

For Steve Reinemund of PepsiCo, "passion isn't style. It's really an inner drive which is so strong that it not only motivates yourself but it inspires others. And I've seen people who've done it charismatically and I've seen people who have done it very uncharismatically. But you can see it in them, and it inspires other people to follow them." It is also perseverance, he added, "the ability to stick with the task through difficult times and pick yourself up and pick other people up."

Jim Donald, former CEO of Starbucks, said: "In order to be successful you've got to have just an unbelievable energy and passion for the business that you're in. If you lose it, it gets felt by every employee of the organization." No one has suggested for a moment that loss of passion had anything to do with Donald's falling out with Starbucks, and we did not discuss what happened there (I wanted his insights from thirty-four years in retailing, most of it in senior management and executive roles). A more articulate and passionate advocate of good leadership would be difficult to find (see chapter 8).

Without passion, don't expect to get through the stressful days ahead of you—all of the tough decisions, delegation, hardships, late-night hours, and crises. I asked Terrance Marks for a single piece of advice for aspirants to the C-suite, and he admitted it was rather simple: "The advice I would give sounds so trite, but it's really true.

Figure out what you love and go do it because you're going to be much more effective doing something you enjoy. And you're going to wind up having to work for a long, long time. Find something that you can really feel passionate about."

Take Less-Traveled Roads

Earlier in this chapter, we discussed the importance of taking risks early. Related to that is the notion that advancement doesn't always equal upward movement. If you have a singular focus on a vertical ascent through the organization, you could miss out on untold opportunities. Broaden your business knowledge by moving sideways into areas with which you are unfamiliar—and get to know the job.

John Kealey of iDirect recently sold his company to Singapore Technologies, so he knows firsthand what it's like to go into unknown territory. He used a climbing analogy to describe business careers. In the early twentieth century, a career trajectory was like hiking up a mountain. You saw the summit and worked your way up, with your eye on the top the entire time. You knew where you were going. "Now, we're rock climbing," he told me. "We're just kind of working our way up the side, not quite sure where we're going or where that next turn is. But if you're smart and aggressive and opportunistic you find your way to the top." While it may not seem to be the fastest way, the most intelligent path between two points may not be a straight line. Remember, there's no elevator to the top.

Executive Summary

It's about you—not your plans. You can hope and wish and plan—there's nothing wrong with doing that—but whether you get to the top is more about whether you want to do the best you can with the task immediately before you. You head upward more quickly through sideways moves than through dogged pursuit of the summit.

Observe those who lead. You will learn a lot by watching your bosses as you progress in your career. If they are good, you will see how to do the same thing—and you should consider asking them to give you advice in your career; if they are bad, you will see what not to do, which is just as important a lesson to learn. In both cases, you will learn how to deal with failure, an important part of your future as an executive.

Play to your strengths, but don't forget your weaknesses. It is important to know what area of business you want to be in and what you are good at. Fill the gaps in your knowledge by doing different jobs, but don't let yourself get stuck in a dead-end one. And never turn down a challenge—budding leaders relish risk, and they get noticed when they do.

Touchy doesn't work in this game. If you can't stand criticism, quit the quest right now. You've got to see it as an opportunity, so welcome feedback. Listen, listen, and listen to what your critics are saying—and thank them for it.

Education never ends. You don't have to secure an MBA (though you are unlikely to regret it), but whatever you do, keep learning. Learn

from others, learn from books, learn from newspapers and magazines. And if you get an opportunity, learn from other businesses.

Work out, sleep in. You will never be able to get to the top and stay
there if you neglect your health and your personal life. Find ways to
keep fit and don't neglect your exercise because you feel you have to
put in an extra hour in the office. And while the way you do it should
be your concern, make sure you align your career needs with your
emotional and family ones, because this is not the kind of life you
want to lead on your own.

If you don't love it, leave it. Without a passion for what you do, you
will lose your commitment and you will lose the support of those who
do it with you.

Chapter 2

Boarding Pass

Climbing the corporate ladder is a long and grueling task, and one of the hardest things to remember as you stay focused on your goal is that it's the path that matters, not just the destination. "I would start by saying that this has been a journey for me," said Arthur Collins of Medtronic. "It's probably an overused phrase, but I don't think it's the ending point that is as important as the journey, and what you learn and what you contribute as you're going through the process."

For Collins, the journey unfolded during his school days. "I always thought that I would like to be a leader of some group that was large, a top group in whatever context," he recalled. "I don't know if it was conscious or unconscious in the number of activities that I found myself involved with that helped give me experience that ultimately would be useful later," said Collins, now in his early sixties. He served as an officer on board a U.S. Navy destroyer, after which he did an MBA at the Wharton School, University of Pennsylvania. "Along the way, the journey was meaningful and a lot of fun."

*   *   *

Leadership skills can be acquired, according to many of the executives I interviewed. Do not be discouraged if your first brushes with responsibility feel unfamiliar. "Many people say you are a born leader or you are not a born leader," Sanjiv Ahuja of Orange said. "But I think there are people who you would observe are learning to be good leaders." Having been Orange's CEO since March 2004, during which the mobile company's customers more than doubled, Ahuja is now chairman. He also works as an adviser to Didier Lombard, chief executive of Orange's owner, France Telecom. To acquire the right skills, Ahuja recommends, "set your mind upon it and get the right role models early on in your career."

Russ Fradin, chairman and CEO of Hewitt, the human resources firm, told me that seeing his recruits learn and grow into leadership roles is one of the greatest rewards of his job. For example, he recalls one of his earlier hires, Gene Hall, as a reserved engineer. Now he's the chairman and CEO of the Gartner Group. "Gene was incredibly shy, but now he's a real people leader," Fradin told me with pride. Anyone can aspire to—and become—CEO material, as long as they have the right tools.

Even as recently as a decade ago, there was a cookie-cutter approach to becoming a CEO—you moved quickly from your functional discipline to general management, acquired revenue-generating responsibility followed by being responsible for earnings, and then went on to garner as much of the pie of each area as possible within the company. Collins said those days are gone: "In fact, if anything, the diversity of backgrounds, skill sets, and types of individuals will probably be even more varied in the future. The cookie-cutter approach to being a CEO, if it ever did make any sense, certainly doesn't today. There are some traits of CEOs, and good CEOs of the future, that will be common, but how you get them and what steps you go through [won't]. I don't think there's a formula that you plug someone into at an early age, and at the end it spits out a CEO."

Regardless of the path you follow, by its very nature, trying to be at the top by yourself makes it a journey with few friendly travelers. "It's a very lonely journey," Goh Sik Ngee told me. Goh, who was CEO of Yellowpages.com for four years, spent about thirty-five years in the public and private sectors, including as director of manpower at Singapore's Ministry of Defence. "You feel like you walk the journey yourself. Whether you're enjoying the positive side or it's something that's negative, you do it because you think that's the right thing to do."

Javier Gutiérrez, president of Ecopetrol, Colombia's largest company, stressed the acquisition of mental strength in the quest to acquire leadership abilities: Be open and always eager to learn; look for ways to integrate knowledge and execution tools; have intellectual curiosity; and "read, read about everything," he said.

You'll have to do a lot of thinking on your feet—it's that kind of job. To help you along the way, the CEOs whom I've met shared their insights into how they might do it again, or the things they kept in mind as they rose to the top and evolved into world-class leaders.

Zigzag Your Way to the Top

"I would strongly advocate to anybody coming up that they don't get caught up [thinking] the fastest way between two points is a straight line," Terrance Marks of Coca-Cola said. "Because if you focus only on your vertical ascent through a function or a general management line, then you're going to miss out on untold opportunities to broaden your knowledge of the business by moving horizontally into other aspects, to other functions you may not be comfortable with. And you have to do it early in your career because later in your career you won't be qualified to do it. Establish those qualifications early, choose wisely, and don't do it on a whim."

Marks continued by explaining that a by-product of diversifying your experience is making connections. "The residual benefit of that is that you network," he said. "And you don't realize you're networking at the time, but if you move from a general-manager role to finance, then you begin establishing connections with an entire function of the organization with which you might otherwise have only a surface-level relationship."

Decisions about job moves are difficult and require serious thought and discussion with a mentor, if possible. Marks had many instances in his career where he had to weigh the benefits of each move, even if it didn't seem like it was part of a direct path to the top. Still, he followed his instincts. "I always had a bias that it would be beneficial long-term and would broaden my breadth of understanding," he told me. "I never viewed them as a step back in my career. I perceived all of them to be moves that would be (a) lateral at worst, (b) increase the breadth of understanding that I had of the business, and (c) in many cases gave me the opportunity to work for somebody that I felt like I could learn something from."

Russ Fradin of Hewitt went so far as to say not only that he recommends making sure your career path is diverse but that it's essential if you hope to make CEO. "I think that people can be successful coming from virtually anywhere within the firm, but it is almost impossible to get to the corner office with a single function or single geography anymore, if you haven't had a variety of experiences on operations or finance or sales," he said. "Frankly, organizations worry about that a lot." When I'm retained to conduct a CEO search, the board invariably specifies breadth of exposure as one of the top selection criteria. Sometimes, you get close to the top too soon and you are stuck in a rat race to the top executive's office. By then, it may be too late to gain the breadth that is required. So start early. As mentioned in the previous chapter, take risks and dive into roles that will give you exposure to geographies and functions that are outside your level of comfort.

"I think [lateral moves] are not only good, they're critical," Steve Reinemund said. "My advice when people are thinking about jobs is to first think about what the job is, not where it is. Is it a challenging job that can be fun to do, that [will let you] learn and contribute? And then think about where does it sit, and is it lateral or is it not, rather than thinking about if it's a pay-grade increase, a promotion, which is not unimportant but shouldn't be the first question."

One way of looking at your experience path is to see it as putting you in contact with people from whom you will learn about both good leadership and bad. And the two can come at the same time, argued Arthur Collins of Medtronic: "First of all, you've got to try to join the best organization you can join. The earlier on you start doing it, the better off you are. Try to put yourself in a position where you're working for someone, or for a group of people who are really good and really stretch you to a degree that you come in contact with leaders who aren't doing a good job. You can learn from that, too. It's not only important along the way to see something and say, 'Well, that really works. Boy, when I get to that point I want to do that or be like that.' The flip side is when you see somebody do something that's just terrible. You tuck that away and say, 'Boy, when I get to that position, I'd better never ever do something like that.'" I've worked for some great executives over the years and I can honestly say that I've learned as much what to do as what not to do from all of them. No one is perfect, and when you see someone at the top make a mistake, learn two lessons from them: (1) how not to make that mistake yourself, and (2) how they rectified the mistake.

Todd Stitzer is the CEO of Cadbury Schweppes. Looking back over his career, Todd said that in the back of his mind he always knew he wanted to be at the top. Now in his mid-fifties, he said: "I always hoped to be a leader of something. I was the leader of a group of legal practitioners in a law firm [he got his BA from Harvard], then I was the leader of the legal department in a company. I was the leader of the marketing department in Cadbury Schweppes. So the CEO thing developed as an aspiration . . . and came after fifteen or twenty years. But wanting to be a leader and accomplish things is always where I started."

I asked Kenneth Hicks of JC Penney—not yet a CEO, but the chief merchandizing officer of one of the most recognized retail chains in the Western world—to look back on his own zigzags. At one point he was head of strategic planning at May Department Stores, having come from the consulting firm McKinsey and Company. "My office was next door to the chairman. I was a senior vice president of the corporation. I was on the back cover of the annual report. But I also knew I wanted to be a merchant. And [the chairman] made an agreement with me that he would train me and develop me.

"So after three years, I moved to the merchandising company. I now had three and a half billion dollars' worth of responsibility, worked with all the divisions, and really got a chance to understand product development, sourcing, and vendors. But I hadn't ever been in a store. I said, 'I really want to get into a store.'" And when Hicks got into a store as the head of store operations, he had responsibility for just half a billion dollars, a big step down. "But I learned how to operate and what to do . . . because I knew I wanted to get here." As it turned out, he never would have become chief merchandising officer if he had stayed in his old job: "The guy who replaced me in the office next to the chairman never [left], and for thirteen years he was head of strategic planning. And that was what he was. I couldn't do that job for thirteen years. It would drive me nuts."

As you're moving through the different stops on your career, however, be careful not to change jobs too fast. Strike a balance by only taking opportunities at the appropriate time and avoid appearing like someone without staying power. "A longer-term perspective is very important," Lee Hsien Yang told me. "I feel that so many people come up and are just looking for the next promotion, and the fifteen or twenty percent more in salary, and they will job-hop. I see CVs where people have been through seven companies in eight years and think to myself, 'This guy's so good, why does he feel it's necessary to do that?' I think the days of lifetime employment are long gone, and at some point in time most of us will switch careers and companies and do something different, but for the ones who do it on a serial basis, I would push very hard in an interview, and you would have to give me a very good reason why this was necessary for your career. You know the current role may not be exactly to your liking, but you have to think about it and see how it builds you for the longer term. Be prepared to take the ups and downs."

All the while, don't get stuck in the present. As we all know, it is easy to get caught up in the day-to-day—how can you not, with e-mails piling up and to-do lists getting longer and longer? But somewhere on your journey, it's essential to look years down the road. One person who knows about that is Nandan Nilekani, co-chairman of Infosys Technologies Limited, which he founded with N. R. Narayana Murthy and others in 1981 after graduating from the Indian Institute of Technology. Nilekani was listed as one of the one hundred most influential people in the world by *Time* magazine in 2006 and was the *Forbes* "Businessman of the Year" in 2007. When we met in his office on the Infosys "campus" in Bangalore, comfortably seated on a sofa in front of his desk, he pointed out that because global business is moving so quickly, *everyone* is trying to figure things out. To stand out from the crowd, you must look ahead and anticipate the future. "You need leaders who can deal with growth, who can manage growth, anticipate, and leverage it," he said. "For most managers this is uncharted territory." So what can you do about it? I asked. Predict the future, he told me. "You need leaders who are able to anticipate the future. If you're running a company, you must have a good sense of where you see the market and the economy and the buying power and the industry five, ten years down the road, and you must be able to say, 'Where do I want my firm to be in this new landscape?' The ability to project forward and get a sense of where the world is going is very important in the growth economy."

Baby Steps

John Swainson of CA, Inc. said it takes time to grow into new roles, particularly if you're going from a specialized one to management. "It's a very interesting journey," Swainson told me. "Particularly for people who are engineers, it involves the progressive realization that it's okay to not do everything yourself, to coming to the point where you realize that setting in place the framework for people to do things to be successful is, in fact, how you get gratification. It's very difficult to see that when you're seeing from the perspective of a young engineer. Those guys are thinking, 'How am I going to create something?'" At some point in the career of an executive on the path to the corner office, he or she moves from being a tactical thinker to a strategic one. This is a critical move. If one does not make this move or is not self-aware enough to recognize that he or she needs to make this move, they will forever be stuck in minutiae and will be frustrated in their attempts to move forward. Swainson continued,

"And what happens, ultimately, is you end up thinking about, 'How do I create the framework, the structure, the organization that will create things because it has the capacity, and it has the people in it?' That's the transition you go through. And in some people it is completely obvious and they jump to it right away—many of these are obviously entrepreneurial people. It's a progression of steps, and at each step you realize that there's another step you could take."

William H. (Bill) Swanson, chairman and CEO of Raytheon, which is a technology leader specializing in defense, homeland security, and other government markets throughout the world, used himself as an example of an engineer turned manager who experienced the same transition on his way up. "As a young man I was very much an introvert," he admitted during our interview at Raytheon's headquarters in Waltham, Massachusetts. "Most people who remember when I started at Raytheon say I was young and inexperienced. But that really changed over time." Being CEO hadn't occurred to him way back then, and for him it was a series of steps. "For me, it became one assignment after another," he said. "I'm going on my thirty-sixth year. I've had fourteen different jobs in this company."

Swanson didn't come across to me as some nervous nerd. In fact, quite the contrary: he sounded like a real people person. His examples were about people, his imagery was about people. That doesn't mean he has lost his engineering bent—he certainly sounded pretty techno-savvy to me as we talked—but he stressed that people mattered.

Steve Reinemund presented an interesting caveat when I spoke to him about contemplating job moves, and he cautioned not climbing the ladder *too* fast, until you have the necessary skills—and to make sure you take the appropriate small steps first. "It's counterintuitive, but sometimes the title you want, the salary grade you want, are not really what you ought to get for your own good," he said. "Because if [you get] a title that is a stretch as an accommodation to a high-potential person, it can actually hurt [your] reception in the organization, your ability to get another job in the organization, the way you're perceived, and the expectations that people have. It varies by company but the title of vice president comes with an expectation of a certain amount of maturity and a little less tolerance for mistakes. It might not be in the best interest of the individual. It might take some fun jobs away . . . because people would say, 'Well, that's not a VP job so I can't offer it to them'—and it almost takes you out of the running. The very thing you may want may not be in your own best interest all the time." While it is tempting to make that transition to your first executive role, assess your gaps and weaknesses carefully. Ask yourself whether you will lose the opportunity to fill the gaps required to make the top spot by accepting the promotion early.

Honing Your Craft

Few people in life are completely satisfied with who and what they are. We all have things about ourselves that we want to improve. And you can—often with the help of a mentor or people who want to help you grow. "If you have the results and the performance, I'll work with you," Russ Fradin told me of young managers. "I don't give a lot of style points. If somebody has an obvious flat spot, a lot of times you can sandpaper a few hard edges. I'll say to people, 'I can work with you on that with sandpaper. If I have to take a chainsaw to it, it's probably in your personality and don't fight it. Figure out how to make it an advantage. We spend so much time focusing on people's faults and not enough time on how to make their spikes real spikes."

Carl Bass of Autodesk said that facing your weaknesses and flaws is what may well help further your career. "It may be that you're a great salesperson or you have key marketing insights or you're a great technical mind," Bass said. "And what happens at a certain point, what keeps you from getting to the next level, is your limitations. The inhibitors are what really get in the way, and that holds you back. There are dozens of vice presidents who are all very capable. What makes the next one the president or CEO? It's usually the people who were able to conquer their limitations much more so than just relying on their strengths. And what I see from many of the people who have this kind of singular fixation on becoming CEO is that they've probably never dealt with their weaknesses before. I also think that they are often becoming CEO for entirely the wrong reason." The wrong reason, in most cases, is entirely driven by ego and short sight. If you take on the CEO job simply to show yourself and others that you have arrived at the pinnacle, you may have set yourself up for a big fall. As an executive recruiter, I am more apt to recommend the hiring of a first-time CEO with potential than one who has failed in the previous job. Failure in many cases occurs because the person prematurely ascended to the role without the requisite breadth required for that position.

Lee Hsien Yang also stressed that your progress will be incremental. "I think many people start thinking they have every right to go up, and the problem with many young managers is life is in a hurry," he said. Rather than trying to jump up the corporate structure as quickly as possible, Hsien Yang stresses the importance of thoroughly learning the basics of a job before moving on: "A lot of people just say, 'Well, I need to do one more year as an analyst, then I can become a VP'. . . . I think you need to think of it almost as sort of a tradesman and craftsman. People come in, and are sometimes happy to try and perfect the craft. And when you have that, then you can move up. Develop a sound foundation, and then you're really good at what you do." There are additional benefits to mastering your current role: "If you are really good at what you do, then all these fears that people have of job security, you never need to worry about. You know what you do well, you can always go out to the market and find a job. But if you don't know what you can do well, and you've been promoted past the point of competence, rest assured that if you go out and put it to the market test, you will have a problem."

Steve Reinemund shares some advice he tells his sons. "My message to both of them and to others that I talk to is to be clear about what it is that you think you need earlier in your hip-pocket skills that you don't have," he told me. "If I were to say in general what would be the kinds of areas where I think people come out a little less prepared than they could be, and if I could do it over again, I would focus more on accounting and finance. That's critical to be able to understand and make it second nature to you. That hip-pocket skill is important." Of course if the person has a background in accounting and finance, then the areas of focus should be on the opposite side of the responsibility wheel—sales, marketing, and operations.

Be Good at What You Do—and the Rewards Will Come

One nugget of insight I received from many of the CEOs I spoke to was something that is easy to lose sight of when your eye is on the top. Wherever you are in your career, do it well, whether the step you've taken is vertical, or horizontal, or in a completely different direction. Even if your current role is, in your mind, a brief transition, do it well. "There are some general themes that would emerge from anybody who has successfully made the transition from an employee to a functional executive to a general manager, and then to a CEO, but I think the first point is that every step along that way you have to be successful," said John Swainson of CA, Inc. He was repeating what I had heard from dozens of other chief executives. Start with your core competence and build a reputation by doing well in that area. Then, broaden your experience by getting exposure to other areas. Cross the chasm and become a general manager, hone your leadership skills, and you will find that you are in line for a top executive role.

However, when you get good at one job, go get another one, and again focus on improving yourself and your skills. Avoid getting stuck in one role. "The advice I give people typically is that you have to avoid becoming so narrowly functionally focused that you don't have the opportunity to understand the business from all its different parameters," Swainson said. "And it's easy to do, to get trapped into a role that you're good at and to be told by your boss that 'We can't possibly have you do something else because you're far too valuable here.' Yet that's what I see as one of the key derailment factors that happen to people often relatively early in their career."

Still, there is much to be gained by projecting the impression that doing a good job, rather than climbing the ladder, is your number-one priority. "I think people should focus on doing the best job that they can and being a good citizen," Cadbury's Todd Stitzer told me. "Stay focused on doing your job. Trying too hard to get noticed is not productive [nor is] vigorous self-promotion."

Coca-Cola's Terrance Marks had a similar view, particularly in the context of what he called "running for office," by which he meant being obsessed with promotion. "Once they sense that your overriding objective is that next job, and maybe nothing to do with what it was you just interacted with that person about, it can really work against you, significantly. I think you can actually lose the support of the organization. . . . A big mistake a lot of people make, and I've seen it firsthand, is they manage up well, they may manage out pretty well, but they forget about managing down. . . . So if you're faking it with respect to the people beneath you, you won't have the foundation even if you do wind up with that job and be successful." In other words, if you treat the people working for you differently from the people you work for or your customers, you will lose the respect and the support of the very people you need to make you successful. The people who work for you should be able to gain value from you through decision making, mentoring, and a strong results orientation.

"My advice isn't to get up every morning and say, 'When will I become CEO, or CIO?' That's the wrong model," Nandan Nilekani said. "I think the model is to get up every day and say, 'How can I add value to my organization?' and 'What do I need to improve? What are the shortcomings I need to address and how can I make a difference?' If you do this day in and day out, you automatically stand out as someone who can lead. So I think the best way is not to even think about becoming CEO, but just focusing on getting up in the morning and adding value." If you work hard, you'll be noticed, and the rewards will come. "I can't think of too many situations where a truly outstanding person has not matured to the top," Nilekani said. "There may be some extreme bad-luck situations, but by and large, if you're good and you focus on doing a good job, there's enough equity and meritocracy out there to take care of your career."

This concept is so important to Lucas Chow of MediaCorp that he called it his number-one rule in his book. "Whatever you are given to do, make sure you do it extremely well," he said. "If you cannot deliver small things, nobody will give you big things." He recalled how he was once group director for quality of SingTel, the pan-Asian telecom company. "Many people would actually shy away from that job because it is a staff function . . . you know, you don't have any real power. You go around and you influence and help and so on and so forth. . . . But I took it upon myself that, look, whatever job you give me to do, I'm going to do it extremely, extremely well. And I believe that if I do my job so well, somebody will take notice."

He said that at the time they were having problems with the quality of the "hotline" customer service. "So I wanted to understand what the problem was, why it was so bad. Was it because you don't have people, or was it that my system was bad?" In time he realized that there were several things that could be done to improve the service.

He learned that as a result of insufficient training, his customer-service representatives were not answering calls promptly. This caused the caller to be in an irate mood by the time the call was eventually answered, resulting in a confrontational conversation and further dropping the morale of the employees at the call center. He placed a mirror in front of each telephone operator and beseeched them to look into the mirror before and during the call. He asked them to make sure that their facial expressions were friendly. It was a simple move, but it achieved the desired result.

In the end, said Chow, they achieved their goal of an answer within three rings. "And nobody would believe that we had done it. In some of the management meetings they say, 'Are you sure?' I say, 'I challenge you now, you make a phone call. If you do not get through, I'll buy you lunch.'" He said that he did not lose any money buying lunch for anyone.

Humbly, Chow observed: "So if you've done an excellent job, I'm very sure that you get noticed. And you get respect not only from the top, but from the people who you work with."

Overcoming Adversity

Of course, the world isn't always as meritocratic as some of these executives make it out to be. As I sought out interviewees for this book, I came across someone whose description constituted a rare string of anomalies. A woman running a construction company was unusual enough, but the fact that her company is in the Middle East and that she is only twenty-seven years old made her especially fascinating. Indeed, that was the word that came to mind—fascinating—when I met Nadia Zaal, CEO of Al Barari, a Gulf real-estate development company. Nadia was the driving force behind the $2 billion Al Barari project, the first Dubai-based mixed-use development to target the premium segment of the real-estate market.

She told me about the inevitable frustrations of "being a woman in this part of the world and being as young as I am." She encounters a lot of condescension from the older males she has to interact with in her job: "For the first, I would say, fifteen minutes it's usually the same thing—they just have that image of me . . . it's not even talking down, it's over-explaining everything, assuming that I don't understand legal agreements or structuring deals—you know it's just like being . . . in Management 101."

Sometimes, she said, she deals with it through some throwaway sarcastic remark. On other occasions, she said, "I'm just very clear. I actually say to people, 'Listen, we're here for this meeting to discuss XYZ. I appreciate that you're trying to get a lot of background information and make sure that I understand . . . but let's get one thing clear,' and then . . . I deal with the issue at hand and just sort of get on with it."

It's another matter when she meets people from Western countries. "I actually find it a great advantage because they're intrigued. When I'm dealing with some of the top architects in the world and the top hoteliers . . . [in one case] the guy actually said to me, 'One of the most interesting or intriguing things for us was working with you, and the fact that you're young and female,' and so I hear that a lot. So it's actually been positive because they are curious to come out and see this young girl who is in the Middle East who's doing these ambitious projects, you know?"

We laughed, even if for many women around the world, dealing with sexism in the workplace is no laughing matter. But her message seemed to be, if you can't beat them, get around them. Zaal is no quitter. After all, she has a city to construct.

Similarly, Monica Woo, president of 1-800-Flowers.com's Consumer Floral brand, has had to deal with the not always subtle strains of sexism. "As a business executive in blue-chip multinational corporations, and now as one of the officers of a publicly traded company, I have to overcome the added challenge of excelling in largely male-dominated environments," she said. With an MBA from the Wharton School, Woo worked in the big global banks Deutsche Bank and Citigroup as well as for Bacardi and Diageo, where women managers were not the norm. "When working and living in Europe, Latin America, and Asia, I regularly contended with less-than-enlightened behavior towards woman executives," she said, a reminder that this, too, is a global phenomenon.

It was, however, from a woman that she learned some of the guiding principles she observes in both life and business. While working for Citibank Private Bank, she had dealings with top private bankers all over the world. One of them had taped to her office wall in Hong Kong a simple piece of paper with eight quotations written in Chinese, called "Life's Eight Ultimates." Capturing "the quintessential values of the Chinese culture," as Woo put it, they espoused self-knowledge, humility, contentment and generosity, urged attention to health, and warned against three pitfalls linked to self. She acknowledged that these were not apparently compatible with the "highly competitive, individualistic, self-promoting, winner-take-all American business culture." Indeed, she remarked, "can you imagine practicing the Eight Ultimates on *The Apprentice*? For sure, Donald Trump will say, 'You're fired!'"

But from these eight principles she has drawn eight lessons for success in contemporary business life (eight being the luckiest number in Chinese culture), many of which echo those that emerged from the discussions I had with other executives I spoke to. They included: life as an endless journey of discovery and learning; the importance of balance between professional and personal well-being; teamwork and the joy of building relationships; patience and resilience.

Get the Lay of the Land

Every now and again, take a deep breath and have a proper look around. Many of the executives stressed that they felt it was important to take their bearings, know where they were and where the company was. Michael Dell had this to say about reacting to new opportunities: "You have to recognize where the growth is happening—today most notably in Brazil, Russia, India, China, and Eastern Europe—and understand that customers in these regions have distinctly different needs from those you may primarily serve today. At Dell, we believe in staying close to our customers to ensure we understand and serve their needs better than anyone else. That's why we've recently launched new operations in Poland, India, and Brazil. It comes down to listening—listen to the customer you're trying to serve before you start proposing solutions."

"I spent the first six months really listening," said Martin Holmish, global chief marketing officer of SAP. "Listening to my clients. Listening to my colleagues. And trying very, very much to understand the culture of this company, the corporate heritage of the company; not to have any preconceived notions."

And when you're navigating your way through a company, always keep an eye on people not only a few steps ahead of you, but a few levels below. You want to keep everything in view and understand and learn what's going on in different areas beyond your own. Part of this involves staying in touch and cultivating relationships with people. "You're going to be working yourself through your own organization and moving from one to another, and naturally you're going to reach out and expand your knowledge base and contact base," Steve Shindler of NII told me. "Reach levels below you, broadening that contact list, and being mindful of the kind of person you may not only interact with today but could . . . down the road." So, while some of the people you come into contact with today may not be relevant to your current situation, think long-term and build relationships with them for the future. All successful CEOs have a network of friends they have known for years and who were not in positions of influence when they initially met them. If you meet someone you recognize has the potential to become a leader, stay close and connected. You never know when that relationship will bear fruit for you.

Ron Williams said: "You have to understand how your organization functions. So wherever you are, you need to understand how people think and their strategic intent two levels from where you sit today, and it's important to understand and work with and help those two levels beneath you, to develop perspective."

CMGI's Steven Crane, who used to work for Pepsi, added: "Get as much exposure to different functions as you can. Don't become 'functionally siloed.' Get around there." He said when he was at Pepsi, "I used to ride route trucks in India, in Pakistan, just to get down into the business." He called it "cross-functional responsibility." Here is an example of a finance executive getting exposure to global cultures and operations that he need not have "wasted" time on in his role. However, he looks back on these experiences as true building blocks of his career.

It's All About Timing

Along your journey, there will be many factors that aren't always in your control, including luck (never), timing (sometimes), and being at the right place at the right time (often). "I don't think there's a single route to [becoming a CEO], and different people will take different routes, but frankly speaking, to be able to become a CEO is more of timing and opportunity," Lucas Chow said. "I look at myself and ask, 'Why am I a CEO right now, and not somebody else?' I don't know that I have extraordinary qualities that other people [don't] have. I credit it to timing, and that I was at that particular point in time." The best you can do is seize the opportunities that come your way, as well as make new opportunities for yourself. But if it doesn't happen exactly when you want it to, remember that, as in all aspects of life, timing and luck play a part. "It's an element of luck," Chow said. "You position yourself and expose yourself for those kinds of opportunities."

Steve Shindler of NII has heard many stories of people being in the right place at the right time. His only advice for doing the same is for people "to be aware of their surroundings and try to put themselves in that situation as often as possible." He then told me of an event he attended at which Wayne Huizenga, the serial, self-made entrepreneur, was receiving an award. "He got up and said, 'Well, I don't know why I'm getting this, because in my whole career I've just been lucky. I've been in the right place at the right time.' And then he proceeded to tell stories about eight different companies that he built from nothing to multibillion-dollar . . . [publicly] traded companies. It dawned on me that there was just a little bit more to him being in the right place at the right time, that his way of acting and drive and passion for his businesses had something to do with that. I think there is some luck involved and a lot of it does come from timing your moves from either one profession to another, or within the same kind of industry group from one company to another, and just making sure you're jumping to a higher level each time and expanding your skill set and training yourself to be a better leader."

However, in the pursuit of placing yourself in the right position for luck to strike, Coca-Cola's Terrance Marks warned against trying too hard to be noticed for the top job. "You certainly don't want to be perceived as running for office. There's a real balance—you don't want to be disingenuous and say, Aw shucks, I could never imagine myself in that role. . . . But at the same time you can't be so consumed by the role that you couldn't look yourself in the mirror in the morning if you don't get it. And your life has to be balanced on, or has to be built on, things that are more enduring than whether you get the next job."

It is a salutary reminder that in this globalized world, you cannot expect one set of principles and lessons to apply everywhere, even with things like a career path or the time required to traverse it. This question of time and timing is one of many examples I encountered as I tried to get a wide perspective on every aspect of the executive experience. So when I asked Raimundo Morales, then CEO of Peru's Banco de Crédito, what lessons he can pass on to the aspiring executive, he stressed that "in Latin America things take a little bit longer" because experience is valued there more than it is in, say, the United States. I asked him, so what does the aspiring executive do in those circumstances?

"Just be a little bit more patient and take the time." This may be hard advice to swallow, but he followed up quickly with this point, which puts a different perspective on it: "Because once you reach the top, your position is probably more permanent than it is in the U.S. and not really subject to fluctuations of the stock price or what happens to your earnings [every quarter]." Morales was CEO at Banco de Crédito for seventeen years, having joined the financial services group in 1980. "It's worth the wait," he remarked.

He also warned that all this waiting and patience should not breed complacency when you eventually get there. "[Some] people feel that they've got the rich job they wanted to have and that they deserve everything and they don't keep making the effort they should have made to continue growing within the organization." Complacency is the biggest enemy of a successful executive. Once you get to the top spot, many families depend upon you and if you give up, you are shirking a major responsibility. You are hired to the position to serve three stakeholders—employees, shareholders, and customers. If you are complacent, you will let one or all of them down.

Interviewing Tactics

For some practical advice, I asked CTPartners' Brian Sullivan for the view from the recruiter's side. What should you do, for instance, when you're preparing for that vital interview, whether with the headhunter or the board? "Always think in terms of who is your audience," he said. "Headhunters want and need a lot of information and will question your results, financial acumen, cultural fit, and may want to challenge you on style and reasons for certain decisions. Board members may want to engage differently on industry contacts, the six degrees of separation, and be more inclined to run a softball interview while they make a decision that is cast in concrete." And then he stressed that central point again: "Most important, think in terms of who is the audience; listen and respond. Don't pre-can anything." Sometimes during an interview, we find that even senior candidates answer questions that require thought instantly. It is clear to an experienced interviewer that he or she has answered a similar question before and is merely modifying the answer to come across as someone who is ready for any aspect of the job. As Sullivan points out,

sometimes the answer needs to be tweaked depending on the perspective of the person asking the question.

What About Pay?

At some point you will need to figure out how to ask for more money
and negotiate—so I asked the executives what they thought. "Think
it through," Steve Reinemund warned. "Compensation is an issue
that has caused more consternation to careers than probably any
other single definable issue, and it's understandable." He added,
"People . . . send messages by the way they talk about compensation
that may [not be intended]. We all come from different backgrounds
and we put a different value on money. Unless you're talking to
somebody who has the same philosophy as you do, you're likely to
upset them." Again, it is important to know your audience. Educate
yourself thoroughly. Speak with friendly executive recruiters and
determine the value of the position. Arm yourself with data about
similar positions at competitive companies. Never be emotional
about compensation but rather make it a fact-based conversation. If
you decide to have a "take it or leave it" discussion, be prepared to
leave. Unless you are in a tenuous situation (then I would question
the reason for staying with the company in the first place), I do not
recommend this route.

So what do you do? "Count to ten before you talk, and be clear
about the implications, and make it worth it," Reinemund continued.
"In a large, successful company it's been my experience that people
don't get abused for their pay over any reasonable period of time, although at any one time they may be out of sync." This is not necessarily true for all companies. Unfortunately, the executives who usually
get the short end of the stick are the ones who have been loyal and

stayed with the company for a long time. If you started at a compensation level that was below market value, there is a chance that you will
remain below market for the duration of your stay. With every move,
take the opportunity to have a discussion with your boss regarding
compensation. This is the best time to have the conversation, not
later on as your boss may suggest. Incentive compensation can and
should be based on how you perform in your new job, but your base
compensation should be based on the role and responsibility that
you are being hired for.

When I interviewed Joseph Lawler, CEO of CMGI, at the NASDAQ-
listed e-commerce company's Boston offices, I asked him what he
thought about recent business-school research that suggested that
stock options for CEOs were not a good idea since CEOs who had a
high amount of stock options as part of their compensation package
tended to take greater risks. He began by acknowledging that C-suite
executives differed in their attitudes toward why they were doing
what they were doing. "I think there are some people who get to the
top because they are focused on maximization of wealth for themselves. In the process of creating a lot of wealth for themselves, they
create a lot of wealth for other people. And I think that works." Then
he described a different model of executive motivation: "I think
there are other people who get to the top because they're effective
with teams. They're good leaders. They have a bigger idea, they're
able to facilitate, coordinate, and collaborate with larger groups of
people."

So how does Lawler see himself affected by stock options? "For
me, it's not just the stock, but it's not that the stock isn't important.
When I walked in here, I negotiated my package coming in the door.
It had to do with a certain amount of equity—that if I was successful
in driving this business, I would make a lot of money out of that. But
you know, the good news for me is that's done. That's over. . . . I now

make decisions that are just good for the business." With the increased oversight by regulatory bodies on stock-option grants and their eventual realization of value, CEO decision making is under major scrutiny. Do not make the mistake of making short-term decisions that can come back to haunt you. As Lawler says, make decisions that are good for the business.

Never-Ending Journey

As you may already know, getting to the CEO spot is just the beginning. Ben Verwaayen, CEO of BT Group, suggested shedding the idea that you're climbing a mountain and that once you're at the top you get to come back down. "That's not at all as I see it," he told me. "I see it as a start of a journey, never as the end of one."

To keep the demands of his role in perspective, Aetna's Ron Williams even applies a similar method to measuring his own growth as he does to growing a company. "You always have to make certain you continue to learn and evolve as an executive," he told me. "One of the rules I try to apply every year is 'Have I done things that make me fifteen percent better than I was the year before?'" While quantitative measures are easy to keep track of, it is more difficult to measure your growth as a leader once you are already at the top. It becomes important to break down your goals into actionable items that will positively impact the result. Williams said by way of an example, "The way I think about it is, if you were trying to grow your earnings fifteen percent, as an example, then what are you doing to actually make yourself a better executive and better understand the environment in which you operate?" Even at the top, you should always strive to better yourself.

In fact, for most people who get to the very top, there is no option but to continue learning. Because, as Bill Nuti, CEO of NCR Corporation, put it, "the skills that got you there are not necessarily the skills that will make you successful as a CEO." Nuti had ten years at Cisco in the earlier part of his career, in Asia, Europe, and the United States, "running large sales organizations and theaters of operations," as he put it. But while what he did contributed to his ability to become the CEO, of course, "there were many, many things I had to learn as the CEO. For example, working with a board of directors as closely as one does as a CEO versus being a number two or a number three or a number four at Cisco is quite different. You're dealing with a group of people who are highly intelligent, highly accomplished, probably very successful, and the aggregate nature of that in a board is significant enough where learning how to work with that group is not something you get, until you get there." There were many areas, he said, where he wished he had had some preparation, one of them being corporate governance—the manner in which a corporation ensures that it is being run in adherence to laws, ethics, regulations, and best practices. "Lord knows, I had very little information, very little training, if any, on corporate governance. . . . That certainly was a skill that I didn't have that I needed to acquire when I got into the job."

Another missing skill Nuti felt strongly about was what he called "external communication"—with the press, analysts, and investors. He said he had been luckier than most, having "grown up at Cisco" where the CEO there, John Chambers, "was kind enough to put me in front of investors in investor conferences . . . and to do the press." Representing the company to shareholders and the media is an important part of a CEO's role, and one that many executives don't get a chance to develop before taking on the role. As Nuti explained, "The way you communicate or become used to communicating with sales and marketing is not the way you communicate with investors and analysts."

Have Fun

"I can't imagine having to go to work every day saying the only reason I'm doing this is for the money or because it's going to get me somewhere where I want to go," Steve Reinemund told me. "I don't think I could do that. I think it's hard, but I'm not saying people shouldn't do it or it's bad to do it, it's hard for me to see how you could get motivated to do that." Of course, Reinemund admitted that not every job he did gave him total satisfaction every day. "When I sat down with myself and said, 'Is this what I want out of life,' I obviously said this isn't what I want to do forever, but I didn't go in gritting my teeth, and once I got to the job in the morning it was exciting all day." I haven't met a successful executive who isn't completely thrilled with his or her job despite the daily hurdles to be overcome. The single reason for that is by the time they get to this position, they have determined the function, the industry, and the job that they enjoy. I have also met many CEOs who always want to have a discussion with me regarding their "next" job. While some of them want to move on because they do not feel challenged, some of them just don't like what they are doing. It may come as a surprise, but there are many CEOs who took the job for the wrong reasons and find themselves in a position that gives them little fulfillment. Before you take the top spot, be absolutely sure that you will have fun and you are not doing this simply to add the role to your résumé.

Executive Summary

There is no single route to the top. More and more, the path to the CEO spot isn't a straight one. Be open to going in different directions throughout your career, even if the new positions don't follow an upward trajectory.

Get good at your job, no matter where you are. Instead of focusing on exactly when you'll land in the corner office, make sure you excel at whatever given job you have. You'll be noticed, and won't be perceived as someone who's just biding her time.

Keep the long run in mind. The business world is changing so much and so rapidly that you must learn to look ahead years down the road, projecting new trends and new directions your company will go in, so you can move along with it.

Take small steps. Allow yourself the space and time to hone your craft, becoming an expert at every stage, and giving yourself time to grow into a good leader. It won't happen overnight, so relish each stop along the way, knowing you'll eventually get there.

The journey never ends. Remember that even when you get to the top, you should always strive to be better at what you do. Don't get complacent, and don't expect the hard work to stop when you become the top dog.

Chapter 3

You Are the Sum of Their Parts

Y ou can't pull yourself up to the top," said Jim Donald, former
CEO of Starbucks, "but you can get pushed up rather quickly.
And if you allow yourself to be pushed by assembling [the
right] team around you, the rest is history."

No one else put it quite that way—Donald has a way of saying
these things—though everyone agreed that you get to the top not
just by being the best, but by being the best team player. And, equally,
the way to stay there is to hire the best for your leadership team, even
if they seem better than you. "The best thing that you can do is surround yourself with people—an entire team of people—in which
each individual is capable of doing your job better than you are,"
Steve Shindler of NII Holdings said.

Sanjiv Ahuja agreed: "Always have your team stronger than you,
individually. Hire people who are smarter than you." He said he
thinks good team building is "the hallmark of a leader."

And when you've got a fine team, start thinking about who will
take over from you and them. Rick Dreiling of Duane Reade sees succession planning as one of his main duties. "The most important
thing that I do is not only my succession plan but the succession plan

for the people who report to me," he said. "I think far too many companies wait too long to have a successor in place."

So how do you do this? As with so many things in good management, you need to strike a balance—in this case between looking for someone who reflects your values and casting a wide net for people who might not be obvious standouts on your team. Dreiling began with a characteristic nugget of truth before expanding: "If we're all honest, you tend to look for something of yourself in a successor." And then he went on: "You're looking for someone who shares your passion for the business, someone who has broad-based knowledge, and leadership skills, or the ability to articulate what they want done, and to get everybody to rally around it. People talk about 'leadership' and it sounds easy, but if it was easy, we would have a heck of a lot more great leaders."

Bill Nuti addressed the fact that often when you get to the top, you are not prepared for it. He says that succession planning "has to include taking those people whom you know, at least on an internal basis, have the ability to succeed you and giving them more exposure to your board of directors, having the courage to even ask a board member or two to mentor your people."

Putting together the right support team takes time and care. But it is probably the most important thing you are going to have to do. Executives who say you are only as good as your team—and they almost all say that—gave their advice on how to go about it.

A-Players Hire A-Players

In a way, the secret is to go back to gym class basics: pick the best players and you're likely to have a winning team (though we also know that doesn't mean you always win). "The most important thing that I've learned is A-players hire A-players," Steve Shindler said. The most likely impediment to that is when leaders feel threatened by those who are coming up and go instead for those whom they do not fear. "In organizations where [the message is] 'I want someone in that job who doesn't threaten my position or who other people might view as being able to do a better job than me'—that is dangerous. It becomes a culture where A-players hire B-players, B-players hire C-players, and . . . people are not the most productive. All the way down the line, everyone has to recognize that there are smarter people coming up with the organization, and that results in getting the most productivity that you can possibly have."

The concern that those A-players you hire might turn around and undermine you is warranted, but only if your team is underperforming and restless—not if it's doing well. Kenneth Hicks of JC Penney stressed that "the [important] thing is recognizing that the people who you're growing and developing are not threats, but supports for you." Unfortunately, executives don't always see their direct reports in this light, Hicks says: "A lot of people are hesitant about the people under-neath, so they hold them down and they don't give them the responsi-bility and they don't train them. Then they can't ever move up." This is extremely shortsighted. Unless you have a strong succession plan and you have people below you to take on your responsibilities, it becomes difficult for your boss to move you up, as she is concerned about the failure of your current role in the hands of an incompetent person.

Shindler wasn't the only CEO I spoke to who uses the alphabet analogy. "There's an old saying that B-players attract C-players, but you have to have A-players attracting A-players," Rick Dreiling of Duane Reade told me. "Because if you think a B-player is going to drag in an A, you're crazy. And once you have A-players bringing in other A-players, it becomes a self-fulfilling prophecy where you create an environment where people want to perform. And they feel they are given the opportunity to perform." This is an illustration that is often used by executive recruiters as well. A-players are those that are both competent and confident in their own abilities to rise in the organization. They are not threatened by subordinates and therefore hire the best and the brightest, looking to fill spots with people who are even more skilled than themselves. B-players are competent but not confident and therefore will always hire and manage people less competent than themselves so that their position is never threatened. C-players are neither competent nor confident.

Someone can be an A-player without being a star—and that's what you should keep an eye out for. John Swainson told me that he takes cues from people's speaking habits. "What I always look for is, how do people talk? Do they use 'we'? Do they use 'us'? Nothing is worse than watching a presentation of somebody saying, 'Well, I did this or I did that.'" So Swainson will always hire someone who is an A-player but is not necessarily an autocratic superstar.

Russ Fradin turned to sports analogies. "Look at the Derek Jeters [of the New York Yankees] of the world. The guy who's going to go out and kill himself every day, but when he hits the big home run doesn't drop his bat and make a big show of it, tends to be the one that people trust. People don't want a showboater, someone who's self-aggrandizing."

Walt Bettinger remembered some valuable lessons about team building from his early years at Charles Schwab. "When I was in the process of transitioning from a small-company entrepreneur to all of a sudden being in this great big company, there were incredible lessons learned about teamwork," he told me. "There was an executive who I have deep respect for, John Coughlan [most recently CEO of VISA USA]. He had been with Schwab a long time. One of the things that John shared with me was about a year after I joined Schwab. He told me, 'When you were running Hampton [the company Bettinger founded in 1983 and which Schwab acquired] you were the best salesperson in Hampton and you were the best person doing 401k discrimination tests and you were the best technologist and you were the best marketing person and you were all these.' Then he goes, 'Now at Schwab you're not the best at any of those things. Now you may be competent at all of them, and that puts you in a unique position, but you're not the best at any of them.' And I think that's an interesting aspect that I try to carry forth as my role has expanded: give up on being the best in anything; you're not going to be. But attract those who are the best. Build your team from those." Bettinger remembers initially taking Coughlan's words as criticism. As a competitive person, he had always striven to be the best. But Coughlan told him to "strive to be the best at attracting others." Bettinger told me, "That was a great lesson."

Rick Dreiling said that what matters most about good team building is what he calls "chemistry": "It's not just about the experience level but it's also about the chemistry that exists." Describing his team-building process, he said: "I pick them all out myself. They have to get along. There is no politics here. There's no infighting. We make our decisions together as a team. And I kid them all: they have six votes, I have seven, but at the end of the day we make it together. Then, we sit down and chat about every major decision. And consequently, you get buy-in at this level that forces the buy-in further down the pipe. I've got to tell you that anyone who doesn't look for chemistry, the ability for the team to interact, is cutting themselves short." Dreiling concluded by saying, "And of all of the things that I would pass on as a piece of advice that I've learned sitting in that chair is: the team has got to fit."

Developing Your Team

Once you've identified the raw talent for your executive team and you are sure you've got the right group chemistry, what do you do? Part of being a great captain is knowing how to bring out each player's strengths. Terry Marks of Coca-Cola distinguished between staff and management roles when he described to me how to develop a manager. To identify leadership qualities, Marks believes in taking someone out of a management role and putting them into a staff role that has few people or sometimes nobody reporting to them. "In a staff role you can't rely on reporting relationships," he explained. "So your ability to influence others really comes into play. All of the skills that are required to influence behavior, you develop in staff roles. The key to a manager's ability to have a successful career is how they behave when they go back to the line management role. What they ought to do is bring everything that made them successful in the staff role into the management role. Because then you'll have people who are motivated rather than just moving. I found this to be a very effective way of determining a manager's long-term success—how successful they are when they're influencing others without the benefit of an organization chart."

As with all the things a good leader has to pay attention to, team building involves renewal. And here, too, the alphabet formula provided the framework for the method François Barrault of BT Global Services uses to decide what jobs and what members of the team are working well, whom to promote and whom to fire.

He began by grouping people into three categories: "A is great, B is average, C is bad," he began. The problem is not the C people (Barrault recommends firing anyone in that category). The problem is the B people, what Barrault called "not good enough to be promoted, not bad enough to be fired." The difference between a B and an A is "the difference between a manager and a leader," he said.

The way he sees it, a B is either a bottom-shelf A or a borderline C. He or she cannot remain a B.

"Why are they Bs?" he asks. Either their job is not critical, in which case change the job, or the person himself is a B, in which case concentrate on changing him. But the B never stays a B. "He either comes with me or he is out." Barrault said you could see how some companies wait until they are on the verge of bankruptcy before they do this, while others are constantly evaluating in this way. "So, the leader is a guy that deals with the uncomfortable zone, the Bs." He does this by one of two means—either eliminating them from the organization or putting them in a position or location where they will perform as an A.

CTPartners' Brian Sullivan summed much of this up when he said: "Sometimes, you can't get everybody on board because it's just not in some people's blood. However, if you set your values up front, articulate those values throughout the firm and especially in the recruitment process, and do not stretch your values no matter how big an impact someone can make, you'll develop a great team."

While it is important to have a team you can trust and delegate to, you are also responsible for maintaining an active leadership role. Kenneth Hicks explained why: "The second part, after you've given them the direction and guidance, is to let them run it and let them know that it's their responsibility. But then come back and check up on them. The expression I use is 'don't let them walk off the cliff.' Let them know that you're there if they really, really need you. But let them know that it's also their decision and don't come in and say, 'Well, here's what I would do.'"

I asked Hicks when he realized he had to let other people make decisions. As with many other things Hicks brings to the C-suite, the lesson was learned during his years in the military. "When I took over my artillery battery—cannons, I had six cannons—I could shoot a cannon better than any of my section chiefs who ran each of the six cannons. There was only one problem: I could only shoot one gun at a time. So what I knew I needed to do was get the other six guns, or all six guns, better than I could shoot, and the only way I could do that was let them do it because if I tried to run the guns, I could only do one at a time. So I pulled back and I learned that I had to develop people who could do their job better than I could ever do their job, by giving them the responsibility. Because if you don't let the person ever grow, then you're going to have to do the job for them forever." So, as I said earlier in this chapter, in addition to hiring A-players, make sure that they are being continually prepared to take on your job.

Assess Talent—and Include Yourself

Many executives said the process of building teams must be exhaustive if it is to be effective. Rick Dreiling was in the middle of a "talent assessment" when we met. "We're evaluating everyone from store manager up in this company [Duane Reade]," he told me. "We're going through all of the merchants, the finance people, and we're identifying who the people are who need to be mentored, the people we think have a future. We're identifying the people who we think are going to be world-class. I've worked in a lot of places, a lot of different divisions where that didn't exist. But this is truly how you find the young people that need to be identified and brought along."

Bill Amelio of Lenovo described a similar review process in place at his company. "We're starting to analyze successful people's careers, noting their experiences, and using this as the basis to model other people's road maps and individual development plans. If we can provide all of our employees with a sense of what it takes to do great work, and show them the behaviors that enable people to execute and excel, then there's a higher probability for success in key jobs," he said. To him, it's all about fulfilling his team's potential and preparing them for the next step in their careers. "It is so important to make sure that people who want to strive for that next opportunity in the company have the right set of experiences to ensure success in their next, bigger role. Experience is essential. Identifying and training leaders is not about who you might like personally or whether someone is a 'good guy,' but whether a high-potential employee is getting the experiences that will help him or her move forward. The job for a CEO is to help provide opportunities and experiences to prepare people to run a major organization globally or even lead the entire company."

It's important to keep an eye out for people with initiative who seek challenges, but often, the onus is on the people in charge to do just as Amelio does—make sure people get the right experience for their future jobs. Bob Reynolds of Fidelity also makes sure to put people in roles that will help them reach their potential. He took an operations person and put him into sales, believing it was a career path that would pay off—and it did. "I thought he had terrific potential because he was smart, people loved working for him. So I took him, moved him to marketing, moved him to sales, you know, and I made sure he got the experience."

And while larger companies may seem to have more resources to devote to succession planning, all companies, regardless of size, should make this a priority. "I think probably not enough work is done in succession planning," John Kealey of iDirect Technologies (a much smaller company than the ones described above) said when he told me about his own company's plan. "We shouldn't say, 'Well, we're a small company and so we didn't [concentrate] on it or focus on it as a team.'" So Kealey spent considerable time building his team and preparing them for bigger roles. When it was time for him to move on as part of the acquisition, he was able to let his team decide on future steps without his direct involvement.

Regardless of where you are in the company hierarchy, remember that people above you are assessing you in this way. If your company has mentoring programs and talent assessments, get in line and show that you want to be a part of it.

Keep in mind that no matter how scrupulously fair and thorough your searches, there will be repercussions. "Succession plans are dynamic," Lee Hsien Yang of SingTel Group said. "I think the risk you have in any succession is once you anoint, or pick the person, whether an internal or external becomes the CEO eventually. And the ones who clearly were considered, who went through a process, and who came out without an outcome, therefore are disappointed. We are all human. People have great expectations." As part of a CEO recruiting process, we always recommend to the board that internal candidates be treated the same way as external ones. It is equally important to give granular feedback to those internal candidates who do not make it. Overlooking someone who thought he or she was the heir apparent, or finding someone from outside the company when others hoped you would hire internally, has consequences that you will have to face time and again. "There will be bruised egos," Lee said. "Sometimes people just leave, which I think is an unfortunate outcome." In an ideal situation, candidates who were in the running were obviously valued as part of the team, and will stay, but it is likely you will lose them.

Diversify

Good executives don't just talk about diversity; they take it to heart. Bill Amelio of Lenovo referred to his team as being the equivalent of the United Nations: "I look at my global leadership team, and when we get together, it reminds me of a meeting at the United Nations, with so many different cultures and nationalities represented," he said.

"I think the strength of our company is that we bring together the best of East and West. The chairman is Chinese and he lives in Raleigh, North Carolina. I am an American living in Singapore. My chief marketing officer is Indian. Our chief strategy officer is Vietnamese. Diversity is a real strength. It is key to innovation, to serving global customers and to differentiating a company and a culture. Successfully cultivating ideas from such a diverse team is a great competitive advantage because you are harnessing the power of different perspectives that are building from the same fundamental strategies."

Goh Sik Ngee, formerly of Yellowpages.com, also referred to his team as "a mini–United Nations," and couldn't emphasize enough how important diversity is. "Our Japanese partners think and behave differently from someone in Budapest or Taiwan," he said. "So you have to learn the art of dealing with them and you cannot do that unless you have some understanding about their culture and their thinking. When you develop your team you also need to develop people who have that kind of exposure. You need people from different cultural backgrounds to come together."

Walt Bettinger of Charles Schwab expands the concept of diversity to include far more than different cultures. "It's a positive if someone has global experience and exposure to diverse cultures," he told me. "They have diverse ways of thinking about things, complementary perspectives and experiences to what other people on the team have. But I don't put it in a global context. I put it in the context of life. When I have formed teams, that's what I've looked for: Where do I get the life experiences? Where do I get the complement?" As an example, Bettinger told me that while five years ago most of his leadership team worked in San Francisco and were from the West Coast, he now has direct reports who grew up and currently reside in different parts of the country. At the time we spoke he was in the process of filling a new position and wanted to make sure it was filled by a non-U.S. resident. He also looks for a range of ages and schooling (i.e., not just people from "prestigious schools").

To Bettinger, who has a summa cum laude degree in finance and investments from Ohio University and completed the general management program at Harvard Business School, his efforts to diversify translate into a better company, with everyone bringing something different to the table. In fact, he used the very table we were sitting at as an analogy to illustrate this point. "I describe it as adding different views to a problem. So here's the example I use with people. If the answers to all the problems that we face are written on the outside edge of this table and we're all sitting in chairs and the one requirement is that all we can do is scoot up and scoot back, well, it matters not how far back I scoot, because I will never see more than some fraction of the solution to the challenges. So my job as a leader is to ensure that my team consists of people with varying life and business experiences that sit in all the chairs all the way around the table. And then my job is to foster a world of openness, transparency, honesty, and vulnerability among the team such that we are willing to share with each other what we see and not hoard the part that we can see out of our peripheral vision." So, while it may be important to opine on something that is outside your immediate span of control, it is more important to hear out the individual who is directly responsible for that function or process. If you constantly make comments from "another part of the table," you will soon find yourself lonely and not part of the team.

Be a Good Teammate

Once you have your players together, be a good captain: "The thing I have always done is to be very straightforward with people,"

François Barrault said. "When I talk to people I never, ever, remind them that I'm the CEO."

Likewise, Terry Marks of Coca-Cola talks about his role as being more like the coach of a sports team than the general of an army. "We have a process that we call 'being in the huddle,'" he told me. "It's not literal in the sense of an American football huddle . . . but the idea is that we call the play in the huddle. It's where we bring together our key leadership—my direct reports and the senior leaders of our business units out in the field in North America. We'll come together to review, debate, and discuss. We're really pushing everybody to share their point of view in an open and unedited way." I imagined that some of the huddles might take place right there in Marks's office, where we were doing the interview. On the wall near the conference table was a whiteboard with writing and numbers on it.

And when those unedited viewpoints come along, show your team spirit by casting aside your ego. "For me, the most important thing is the ability to team," BT Group's Ben Verwaayen told me when we met in his office in central London. "In order to team with somebody else you need to be able to say, 'Sorry, I'm wrong. You have a better idea.' You need to have a laugh and you need to have a fight. The prime way you can have a fight is with a smile on your face, where you have a constructive battle."

Team spirit resides in one important further commitment, according to Marks. Once the talk is done, you all do the same walk. "When we break the huddle, when we leave there, everybody runs the play. And the analogy is—it's a really good football analogy—is that if the quarterback thinks you're running a post and you run a curl, well, you're going to have an interception. So, if anybody misses their assignment, we've blown it, and you've let everybody else around you down, not just yourself." This is an extremely important concept that I learned from a CEO I used to work for. He always said that it was okay to disagree with others inside the boardroom but once a decision has been made, then everybody exits that room as one team. Don't walk out rolling your eyes, waiting for the initiative to fail so you can say that you were the one who disagreed with it in the first place. Marks said, "The whole concept of complaining about the idea after the fact is countercultural. It's really an indication of bad faith, of going in the hallway and complaining about the idea, or the decision that was made in the room. Your opportunity to do that is in the room. Say it loud and clear. 'I think this is a bad idea, okay.' Well, when we [reach] the decision, the door opens, we all leave. It may have been a bad idea in there but now it's the plan."

Of course, it's a challenge to be a cooperative member of a team while at the same time maintaining a role of authority. Ben Verwaayen explained how he copes with that: "I am not the kind of person who says, 'Give me your input,' then closes the door and then comes out saying, 'Here are the Ten Commandments.' That's not how I'll do it." He gathers his team around the table and discusses the issue before offering his guidance. "Then I say, 'Okay, here it is. This is what I think we should do.'"

Joseph Lawler of CMGI is adamant that someone has to lead: "When you have a lack of clear direction, what you do is just have people sitting around, smart people, talented people sitting around waiting for somebody to bark the next order. It's no way to run a business."

If the decision goes wrong, however, don't revisit the argument and find someone else to blame. Kenneth Hicks of JC Penney insisted that a good team leader never says or feels "It wasn't me, sir." This is more than accepting that the buck stops with you. It's about making your team work better and getting the outcome you want, and it works at every level of management. "If you're not willing to be yelled at or criticized because of something somebody who works for you did, didn't do well, but you could have done better, you shouldn't be a leader," he says. "You have to realize that you're going to have people who you work with who are not going to be perfect, and you have to help them grow and develop." He adds that "if you can't do that, if you can't take the responsibility, the pressure of leading people, if you don't like working through others, and you just say, 'Well, I can do that better than them,'" you should look for another career trajectory. "You have to work through others," he emphasized.

For example, Hicks said, you might have put together an ad and it didn't work. And the conversation with someone higher up could go something like this: "'Jeez, that was a terrible ad.' 'Yeah, it was bad.' 'Why did you do that?' You can't say, 'Well, I didn't do it. The person who works for me did it, and he's stupid.'" Not only should you never do this, you shouldn't even be thinking it. This doesn't mean, however, that you just take the criticism on the chin and leave it at that. "You are responsible for everything your people do. So now what are you going to do about it?" Hicks asked. One option, of course, "is to go down and say, 'Okay, you wrote that lousy ad. Get the hell out of here.'" More often than not, Hicks said, it's the wrong move. After all, the buck stops with you. If the performance continues to be poor after you've had that discussion, then you have a weak link that needs to be removed.

For Lawler it is an important part of your own growth as a leader to have brushes with failure and see the limits of your team. It helps you understand your own limits and forces you to address them. "As soon as you figure out you can't do all this yourself, and you have to assign, allocate responsibility to somebody else and they screw it up, what you do about it has as much to do with your development as anything else." The inexperienced leader pulls it all back to him or her and says "Forget it, I'll take care of it myself." You would have missed the opportunity to strengthen yourself as a leader and also to provide strong support and leadership to your subordinate. Lawler continued, "So [you should be] continuing to give people more and more responsibility so they, too, have to entrust others to get something done, how they learn the disciplines of being clear about goals and objectives, delegating, following up on all of those things. What do you do when something goes right? What do you do when something goes wrong? Those are tremendously important skill sets. It helps you pick better teams."

Take One for the Team

Of the many functions of a solid team, one of the more important aspects is support. If your team is strong, it'll follow you throughout your career, and serve as a cheerleader and support system. Terry Marks of Cola-Cola stressed this as a reason to cast a wide net, making contacts in different departments. "You're building a stable foundation upon which you can build," he said. Marks worked with people from many aspects of industry, something he told me he was grateful for in retrospect. "I never thought of it as networking, but the residual benefit of all of that was that I did network quite a bit, and it dawned on me later, when I found I had a significant amount of support from various functions, that it was because I'd actually interacted with a lot of those people. I was sensitive to their needs and the contribution that they made."

But as the old adage goes, there is no "I" in team, and the only way you'll get that support is by being a great team member yourself. Russ Fradin of Hewitt told me that in a team you want cheerleaders who'll root for you, but you have your duty to them, too. "The more people you have in your rooting section, the better you are," he said. "And you do that not by being political, but by helping people." Chances are, they support you because they know you pull your weight—you're the person who stayed an extra hour, or helped someone out when he was having a tough time, or filled in for someone. "I think that you build goodwill and trust over a long period of time," Fradin said.

Bill Swanson of Raytheon took this idea one step further when he spoke unabashedly about love. And he wasn't the only executive I spoke to who was willing to speak frankly about feelings. "Love is all about giving of yourself," Swanson told me. "Leaders are willing to make sacrifices, and their teams know that instantaneously. Let's say we're doing a proposal. Somebody has a daughter who's doing a recital. Somebody has something else that's important. I find that leaders will go and cover for the individual. I find that leaders will take a shot for their team. But that's what leaders do because they love their teammates. They love the people who work with them, and they do anything to help them be successful. And they don't take the credit for it."

Life at the Top Doesn't Have to Be Lonely

Once you get your corner office, your team-building work will pay off. The CEO spot can be a solitary one, but it doesn't have to be. "I don't think it is a very lonely job, because in all circumstances I have been able to find people, colleagues who I can share the burden with," Lucas Chow told me. "I am very fortunate that I [was] able to find like-minded colleagues who share the same kind of passion. These are the people that most probably appreciate the pain, the suffering that I have been put through."

Ben Verwaayen recalled the point that if you want to make it to the top, it isn't about your ambition but about teamwork. "We live in team sports," he said. In business, "ambition is only acceptable if it's refracted in bringing other people along, bringing a solution along. If it is pure personal ambition, please run the hundred meters and win the gold medal. You could be absolutely solely focused on yourself. Be a scientist and find a new cure. You could [win] the Nobel Prize and you could be totally on your own." In fact, Verwaayen has always been a bit of a team player. He grew up with five brothers and sisters in a village in central Holland and organized his high school's first student parliament. During his army training, he launched an unauthorized union among fellow conscripts to push for better wages and conditions.

If working on your team is as much a priority for you as making money for your company, you'll have more than just good financial results to be proud of. Bob Reynolds finds this payoff has huge dividends in his role at Fidelity. "You have a lot of pride in the people who work for you to see them grow and expand," he said. In fact, this pride was an unexpected perk of the job. "Some of the greatest pride today is seeing some of the old team move on and do other things, big things. That was one of the things I didn't anticipate. As you're going through the process you don't totally realize what you're accomplishing because you're just trying to get after it day after day after day. And, in hindsight when you have a chance to reflect, like when I made the decision to step down, it suddenly hits you because you're getting e-mails and letters from people about how you affected their lives. Being a part of something that turned out to be great was something they'll never forget."

So, how do you know you've created a strong team? Perhaps in a bittersweet way, you know you've done well with your team by seeing how it fares in your absence. John Kealey of iDirect experienced this when he announced he would step down. "It's been very rewarding, because my team has really come together well," he told me. "A test of it has been since I announced my resignation, and I went to the team. A few days afterward, we held a two-day offsite meeting to discuss the transition. The first day we talked about it, I said, 'What are you going to do now, because I'm not going to be here, right?' Then the second day I stood up and I said, 'Just so everyone really believes that I'm not going to be here, I'm leaving.' And I walked out of the meeting at eight-thirty in the morning. I had someone who was facilitating for me, and he said that really hit them where they thought, 'He's serious!' This really helped shape their behavior change in approaching the issue. They had to take over. Over the next few months, I removed myself from the process of leading the company and made sure that I was more in the background and just helping them where I felt that they needed help. But it was really powerful to watch them come together as a team, get their second-quarter numbers and get momentum."

If you've been a great leader, you'll have created a team that is well equipped to find someone new who can fill your shoes and continue the legacy you worked hard to create. This is exactly what Kealey's team did. "They got real clear about what they wanted in a new CEO, and what they felt they needed in a leader, and they helped select the new CEO. I was very proud and felt great about them."

Executive Summary

They're on your side. Hire the best people because you are only as good as they are, and if you feel threatened by good people below you, you will foster a culture in which everyone hires someone weaker than themselves. In the end you will be the loser. Instead, make sure you build an A team out of team players rather than a B team out of A-players.

Keep thinking about who's next. Succession planning is an important leadership role and it can't be done in an ad hoc manner. Bring in proper talent assessment systems—and include yourself in them as you move up toward the C-suite. While you might want someone like you, cast your net wide and keep your mind open. Even if it makes for disappointment, do not be afraid to hire from outside.

Have regular makeovers. Work out what good potential leaders need and find ways to give it to them—spread them around the company, assign them to new functions to fill their skills gaps, and send them on courses. And when someone's in the wrong job, change the job or the someone—don't dodge the issue.

Make your team look like real people. Diversity is not about human rights. It's about running a good company, and you can't do that if you don't draw on the range of talents, experience, knowledge, and backgrounds necessary to function in a globalized marketplace.

You're only the captain. There's a whole team on the field and a good captain brings them all along on every play. Agree on a game plan together and argue it out before you go onto the field. And when you do, everyone should be signed on. No one, least of all you, should say they didn't agree with the plan in the first place.

It might be tough at the top, but it doesn't have to be lonely. Your team will support and root for you if you do the same for them. That way you won't go home alone after the game. And when the time comes for you to move on, they will keep it together—if you've set an example of good leadership.

Chapter 4

Corporate Bonds

The Art of Networking

To say that Nadia Zaal is busy is an understatement. "I hardly sleep," the CEO of Al Barari told me when I met her at her company's home base in Dubai. It's not that she's stuck in her office or in her company's conference rooms all the time to make sure the company's strategy is being properly executed. "Apart from the actual 'real work,' I would say a third of my time is taken up by networking," she said. "It's very important."

Like many of the executives I spoke to, Zaal maintained that networking is an indispensable tool and worth the time that goes into it. To some people it's a loaded term, suggesting insincere schmoozing. "It has a positive and negative connotation," Steve Reinemund of PepsiCo told me. "My reaction to the word has more of a negative connotation, but the principle is a good one. If people are networking in order to get contacts to further their careers, that's bad. If they're doing it to sell an idea or the effectiveness of the organization, that's good. And quite frankly, it's critical in large organizations to do it."

This is the one area in which I found more diversity of opinion than agreement, save for the fact that most executives thought some form of networking was essential. The key to effective networking, it seems, from the range of views on the subject, is knowing what you want from it and developing your own networking style. In essence, it is a tool for expanding your contacts and deepening relationships with your peers. It can also create opportunities for you to find formal and informal mentors and others from whom you can glean information and advice. Indeed, mentoring and networking often overlapped in my conversations with executives.

Probably the most telling of those conversations that touched on networking was with Jim Donald, former CEO of Starbucks. Donald told me how he came to work for Sam Walton, founder of Wal-Mart, a year before the legendary retailer died from cancer. At the time Donald was running the western states food-store chain Albertsons, and Walton called him and said he wanted to see him. (In fact he wanted to persuade Donald to run Wal-Mart's new grocery division.) He said he would fly to Phoenix, where Donald lived, and asked him to meet him at the airport. Donald couldn't believe it, but he went to the airport and sure enough, "there comes Sam boppin' off the plane with his Wal-Mart hat on and his fanny pack of cancer medication. And we spent the day [together]. He said, 'I want you and your wife to come see God's country.' And I said, 'Where might that be?' And he said, 'Bentonville, Arkansas,' and so I said, 'When?' And he goes, 'I'll have a plane pick you up Friday.'" In three years, Donald grew Wal-Mart's fledgling grocery division from 6 stores to 146.

I asked Donald why he thought Walton wanted to see him so badly. "Of all the things that you learn and all the things that you do, networking has to be a critical component of your steps to wherever you want to go. You've gotta be able to network," he replied.

He went on to tell me how Sam Walton learned about him. "My name came across his desk in this manner. There was a fellow named Drayton McLane [who today owns the Houston Astros baseball team] whose company was servicing our Albertsons account. My grocery head of procurement threw [McLane's company] out for reasons I don't know, and I wasn't real happy about that, so I had him put them back in. It was just a matter of doing what's ethically right," Donald explained.

"So our [guy] puts them back in, and I go about my business. Well, apparently this touched Drayton, and when Sam asked Drayton about who was out there in the supermarket business that he knew, he said, 'Well, this guy Jim Donald, and I can't say I know him, but this is what he did for my company. He treated us right.' And that's how Sam came to call me."

Many an executive has made the point abstractly—do the right thing and eventually it will work its way back to you—but few have been able to tell such a good story to illustrate this, nor the point that networking and mentoring are closely connected. For once Donald went to work for him, Walton quickly became a hugely influential person in his business career.

"I think networking is extremely important, both in terms of initiating a job contact or becoming better leaders," Nandan Nilekani, cofounder and CEO of Infosys Technologies, told me. Infosys is one of the largest IT companies in India, and Nilekani undoubtedly used his networking skills to meet people along the way who could guide him as he grew Infosys into the $3.1 billion company it is today. "It's not just about getting something, it's also about using and enhancing your ability to influence," he said.

Bill Swanson of Raytheon put an even finer point on it. "CEOs who understand the power of the social network and the business network are going to be the ones who understand the future," he said. When he looks at his contact list, he asks himself, "How do I knit together all of these critical, diverse capabilities to make the whole better? People who know me know I'm always connecting dots or putting the links of the chain together." Your success, not only in climbing the ladder but in building a leading company, is as strong as the people you can call upon, because these are the people who will advise you, help you out, and whom you can appoint to key positions in your company in the future.

"As you start to get up higher in the pyramid, you realize that your networking ability, and your worth to the entire network, is what provides the keys to the kingdom," Swanson told me. "Your network helps you get recognized. Your network helps you be somebody who people want to have on the team, or you want to do business with, and that they feel good being associated with."

Sometimes the network delivers some pleasurable surprises. During our interview, Swanson excused himself while he took a call from Robert Kraft, the owner of the New England Patriots, asking him if he wanted to attend the Patriots' game against Indianapolis that Sunday. It was probably the hottest sports ticket of the year (both teams were unbeaten at that stage of the season). But Swanson said he had had to turn it down—he had a meeting that day (yes, a Sunday!) of the board of directors of another company where he was a board member, and duty came first.

Beware the pitfalls of networking, though, because experienced people can tell in a split second if you're just in it for yourself. When I asked Russ Fradin of Hewitt if one should look at networking as an "I scratched your back, you come and scratch mine" sort of arrangement, he said no; it's just about "doing good things." That way, people trust you. Networking is a nebulous area; one false move and you've botched a relationship, but if you treat your peers and colleagues well, and do good things as Fradin put it, you'll have a healthy network in no time.

Here are some of the networking tools today's most powerful CEOs around the globe use to keep their companies and careers robust.

Thinking Networks

In today's world of proliferating networking groups and online networks like LinkedIn.com, it's easier than ever to include people in your circle. Diversity is a strength in a network—people from inside the company, outside the company, from different departments and industries. And as your career and life changes, so will the people you call upon. "There are functional mentors that can help you understand accounting or supply chain or something like that, and then there's the broader life mentors who help you sort out what's really important to you in life, and how you balance the purpose of living to begin with, with work and family," Steve Reinemund told me. "And those are mentors that are, frankly, the more important ones and the harder ones to find. And they are likely to have lifelong influences on you, and I've been fortunate in my life to have a number of those people. Sometimes they come and go in chapters of your life, and other times they carry over for a lifetime."

Networking is not just about calling someone to help you get a job. You want to always be learning, gaining insight, and, ultimately, becoming better at your job so that you can better serve your company, employees, clients, and shareholders. The more people you have in your universe, the more you can learn. "Networking is really important. You get a much better perspective, you get challenged in your thinking by knowing people in other places," Carl Bass of Autodesk told me.

John Swainson of CA, Inc., who previously worked at IBM, shared that perspective. "I'm very proud of the fact that I have a very broad range of relationships with people across the industry, both people who had worked for IBM at times and people who have never worked for IBM," he told me. "That's been very useful to me both in expanding my view and ultimately being successful in this job. As you climb the ladder, having established a set of relationships with people is incredibly important."

"Networking can help open different perspectives to you," Sanjiv Ahuja of Orange told me. "It is very, very critical. Some people work very hard at it, and to some it comes naturally. Everybody should do it."

Joseph Lawler of CMGI stressed the fact that networking works both ways: "It's building relationships, it's learning from those people. You'll bump into those people another time in your life. There will be a time when you're on a particular assignment, when you can bring value to them. You know, it's funny how it works the other way: when you pick up the phone, and it's not to call and ask them, Can I make a sales call on you in person, but, I met an interesting person that does something that I think might be of interest to you. That's how good networks are built. Networking is really staying connected to a broad constituent of people. So you can help them, maybe they'll get to help you."

Networking Is Knowledge

Bill Swanson gave me a very evocative analogy for networking, inspired from trips he took to Taiwan. On one of his visits he went to the National Palace Museum in the capital, Taipei. "The curator took me to the basement, and [I] realized that they could change the historical exhibits in the museum every three months, and you would not see everything in your lifetime," he said. "That blows you away. They had all of this knowledge way back when, and in that historical system, knowledge was power. The porcelain or bronze was kept in a closed society in ancient times—information wasn't shared. It hit me that when you run a company, you want people to have knowledge. You want to give that up because if you do, the whole knowledge base is going to rise. That's what networking is all about."

Nandan Nilekani took that thought one step further, and suggested that today's world is less hierarchical, and networking is an essential part of leadership. "Leadership is not just top-down, it's becoming much more diffused," he said. "It's much more network oriented because there are a lot of people who you need to get things done who don't work for you. So how do you give them orders? How do you influence them? How do you get aligned? I think that's a very strong ability."

Even within your company, Nilekani, continued, the hierarchy is not as distinct. "Ideas could come from anyone in the organization, and in fact, it's more likely to come from a youngster than some older guy, and it's more likely to come from someone in the front line of the customer than somebody sitting in this office. Therefore your model should allow the free flow of these ideas."

Swanson said he thought "CEOs in the future are going to have to be network specialists." Due to the new corporate structures and governance, CEOs have to be more nimble and versatile in their dealings with people. "We're required to do so much today. I look at what I have to do today and what I did four years ago, and the demands of investors, boards, regulatory people, and the demands of the political process. They are such that you have to become more and more of a generalist."

Where Does Your Network Start?

For some of the executives I spoke to, networking began quite early, without their really knowing that was what they were doing or that there was a name for it. "Networking started from my school days," Goh Sik Ngee of Yellowpages.com told me, and he was fortunate enough that his classmates went on to influential positions. Indeed, many of the CEOs whom I spoke to maintain friendships with people from much earlier in their lives, even before the C-suite came into view.

Once you do get into a company, don't waste a moment. "The first day you walk into a business, you should start thinking of how you can have a broader net," Steve Reinemund of PepsiCo told me. At the very basic level, you're amassing people who can get to know you, and the caliber of your work, so that your network will naturally be full of people who can vouch for you. "It's helpful for all young people as they're moving up in their careers to have a network of people who'll say, 'Hey, give that guy a try, he's pretty good,'" Reinemund told me.

To Lucas Chow of MediaCorp, there are two different kinds of "networking." One is purely social, and the other is for business. "I know of people who show up in every single party and so on, but they're not very effective businesspeople," he said. "They can't pick up the [phone] and say, 'Hey, look, I need your help on this particular deal or something.' They can't do that. Yet there are people who are very effective in networking, and when they are in need, there are people who will step forward. It goes back to what I call 'emotional deposits,' or putting away favors, and whether your networking includes emotional deposits, and how sincere and genuine you are." Chow went so far as to use his participation in this book as an example. "I'm actually giving you an emotional deposit," he said. "I'm agreeing to this interview, so I have deposited some emotional elements with you to seal our relationship. At the end, for example, if I need you to autograph my book, I'm sure you will. That's an emotional deposit, and that's also networking."

Goh Sik Ngee of Yellowpages.com sees networking in a similar light—a reciprocal relationship. "Part of networking comes naturally, but if you do not invest, it will not be effective," he said. "I think a relationship is built when parties are able to help each other. It's not simply 'I know you, we had lunch together. Tomorrow, if I need you to help me with something, I will give you a call and you will help me.' That kind of relationship is not strong, and the help you get may not be, either. If you want the network to be powerful, you have to invest, and find opportunities to help people. I treasure relationships with certain people who have helped me in one way or another in my life."

My next question for him, as yours might be, was, What does a young manager bring to the table, and how can he help someone above him? "It's a matter of finding an opportunity," Goh said. "It doesn't have to be a crisis. Sometimes it's a small help, even simple things such as visiting someone in hospital if they are sick. But I will remember, and the next time that person calls me, I will render my help to the best of my ability. I think that is human nature. Someone helps you and then you remember the help you received from that person."

Russ Fradin of Hewitt agreed that "the worst phone call is calling somebody that you need something from, and you've never done anything in particular with them." Like Chow and Goh, Fradin thinks networking is about cultivating genuine relationships. "It has to be for legitimate reasons, that you really care about people," he said. "I can almost smell it when somebody's too ambitious and they're just in it for 'me.'"

Within your company, try not to limit yourself by just thinking about networking as a way to move up. And once you do get to the top spot, it's still as important as ever. Carl Bass of Autodesk, for example, uses it to help offset a rather paradoxical phenomenon of the CEO. "The higher you rise in an organization, the less information you have easy access to," he said. "And you have to go out of your way to get untainted information." The week I spoke to him, he already had three lunches planned with people with the express goal of networking. And, he said, "if you looked at the organization chart, they are probably three or four or five levels away, but I know [them] to be great people who have good insights about what's going on in the organization. I go out of my way to maintain those relationships. The more you can do it, the better off you are."

Throughout his career Bill Amelio of Lenovo has also cultivated relationships with people outside his department. "It's great if you have people in the organization who can tell you the truth no matter what. I have always been fortunate to work with people who were willing to give me feedback—even if they were not my direct manager. I have had people who would tell me if something was out of line or not quite right because they wanted me to be successful and knew that honest, direct feedback would help me execute and achieve."

One of the biggest challenges is the inherent isolation at the top—sure, you'll surround yourself with a team you can trust, but the help and support you can get from people outside will be invaluable. "It's good to know many different CEOs, leaders, or executives in other companies," Bill Amelio told me. "My Rolodex is thick, and I can call almost anybody in any company. These relationships are incredibly valuable and meaningful. It's a fabulous thing."

Carl Bass recommends developing a network with people outside the company, and maintaining those friends because their career paths may well mirror your own—and you can look to one another for support. "I think it does get harder and harder to have certain conversations within the company, [when] you need someone to bounce ideas off," he told me. "And it's great if you can get someone who's living through the same job but at a different company. There's a whole bunch of challenges associated with being the COO, and I was the COO for a number of years at Autodesk. During that period of time I developed a handful of relationships with COOs who are now all CEOs. It was good to share the challenges of being second in charge, but also of the transitions [that] in many ways [are] so unique and at the other hand similar." Bass now meets with a group of CEOs once a quarter. "I love talking to people who had similar jobs in other companies, because some of the things we take for gospel they don't, and vice versa," he told me. "Having a networking group of people in similar roles is invaluable."

Of course, as Steve Shindler of NII made plain, you are not about to call up peers and tell them confidential business information and get them to make decisions for you. "It's not that you call them up and say, 'This is the difficult situation that I'm facing today' and provide them with the gritty details, but it's more at a higher level," he said. He asks questions such as: "Did you ever find yourself in a situation where these kinds of forces were playing at one another, and how did you deal with it? Can you give me your sense of the business environment we're in right now? What are some of the levers you pulled, or ways that you made decisions in the past to deal with those things?" The strongest people in Shindler's network can offer support on a range of issues, not just the ones he faces in the boardroom. One of his friends, for example, is his age, has family and kids, has had similar roles at another company, and has gone through restructurings. "We've done some business together, and we get together a few times a year. We've built up a friendship and a bond where we can turn to one another, not to make decisions for each other, but sharing enough information without detailed nonpublic information to get a general sense of how they might respond or react. And it's a good sounding board."

Finding Venues

So where do you network? Do you join trade organizations or clubs and make sure you also talk to people on airplanes? Some executives said they believe it's a more organic process. "People can do as much networking as they want to," Carl Bass said. "I would look for an organized group. If they're a CFO, there are those groups. COO, there's groups which do that. The other way I maintained [my network] both before and now is through things like industry associations in which you participate in those with other executives who are at similar levels."

You don't want networking to feel like a job, so choose activities that overlap with personal interests in which you could also meet people and learn valuable skills. "It's good to maintain the right balance, because if you do too much of it, you're not focused on the job," Lee Hsien Yang of SingTel told me. "And most of us do some volunteer work." Lee is the former chairman of Singapore's Science Centre board and works with other not-for-profits. I asked him if volunteer activities will aid a young manager at work, and he said it didn't per se, but that "it really builds a network, and for the company and for you to be seen as a responsible member of the community, that's part of the respected role that you need to play. If you don't play it, you don't pull your weight, [and] people don't view you in the same way."

From Network to Mentor

As we have heard, expanding your network and identifying mentors often happen in tandem. "It should be someone who has been through the wars who has a balanced perspective on their own personality and impact on the process," Todd Stitzer of Cadbury

Schweppes told me. "I think sharing with other CEOs who aren't in the same competitive space that you are in is a good thing. People can recognize the same sorts of challenges." And while you should never discount the value of your peers' feedback, obviously the more experienced your mentor is, the more he or she can draw upon. "I think when you get in a high-pressure situation and you're an adrenaline junkie, you sometimes think the path is always straight up the hill, but that's not necessarily the case. And speaking to older, wiser, experienced people can give you a perspective that you may not have appreciated," Stitzer said. "It's important to talk with people who have lived through the experience and can give you some wisdom and comfort as you seek to create your own path."

When Joseph Lawler of CMGI reflected on his career, he said forcefully, "I wish people had worked harder at aggressively coaching me. I think people spend too much time not wanting to ruffle the feathers [of people they see as having high potential], being careful about too direct feedback, when in fact the best people take the toughest feedback and truly do something with it. I wish people had been more blunt with me."

Bill Swanson told me that one of the most effective ways he reached out to a mentor was simply by asking questions, and he urges young managers to do the same. "I found out early on in my career something that really helped me: there should be no fear whatsoever about asking a question." In 1983 he was thirty-four, and distinctly remembers the manager for the Saudi market. "It was a fascinating world of international business, and I would just go by at six or seven at night and talk to him," he recalled. "I would say, 'Can you tell me how you do business? How do you develop the relationships? How does that work?' People have a tendency not to ask questions because they think it's a sign of weakness, but to me it's a sign of strength. And as a CEO, you better ask questions."

Lawler reinforced his view that there is not enough robust criticism around: "Mentors are really hard to find. But look for them, they're invaluable." I asked him where to look and how you know when you've found one. "You know, I guess my advice is, look for the people who have been there and done that. It's the people—you know, the safe avenue is to pick a peer who is the same age with roughly the same experience who you think is a coach. That person can coach you in certain things. But they, like you, don't know what they don't know.

"So look for somebody with a very different background. Very different skill sets, who still gets the opportunity to kind of observe you. But probably has a different, broader, larger responsibility. And is most likely somewhat older than you are and has a little more time."

Not everyone likes a mentor, of course. Arthur Collins of Medtronic said that apart from in sports, "I don't think I've ever had a coach. I think there have been people along the way who have acted in the role of a mentor. I know that works great for a number of people. I mean, it's just not in my DNA to have an executive coach. I'll go to individuals if I need counsel, but I'll pick the individual depending on what the subject is I want to get counseled on."

Networker Beware

When seeking a mentor, don't fall prey to the first person who pays attention to you, no matter what exalted position they may occupy and at what prestigious company. Just as you pick your friends, pick your contacts and those in whom you want to be investing time very carefully. "Sometimes as a young person, it's intoxicating to breathe the air atop and be a little blind to the underpinnings of where a leader comes from," Steve Reinemund said. "I think some people mistake a mentor for someone who may be a self-serving manipulator. That's a pretty caustic way of describing it, but there are many leaders who prey on young people for their own benefit."

When I met with Reinemund, I noticed that he used the term "moral compass" as the first thing to look for in a role model or mentor as you network your way through your career. It underscored the idea that the people you seek for guidance shouldn't be based on pedigree or résumé or their ability to help advance you to the next step, but that any relationship should be based on a shared value system. "In my experience, those people who have faith but have a lot more experience and have demonstrated a pretty good track record of balancing their lives are the ones I'm attracted to," he told me. "Because I want to find out how to do what they did, and how to balance it in the way they did it and benefit from things they would've done differently. And I've been encouraged by them in the process of realizing you're going to make mistakes." This way, not only do you respect your mentor, but you will hopefully stay out of harm's way.

In a sense, when you are out meeting people and getting to know your bosses and colleagues, use the same measuring stick you'd use on yourself in evaluating whether you can trust someone. "Sometimes it's hard to see the fundamental underpinning of a person from a distance," Reinemund acknowledged. "We're all dealing with human beings, people who make mistakes. But I think if people start with a strong, demonstrated—not articulated, but demonstrated—set of balanced spiritual beliefs, you have a better chance."

Getting back to Lee Hsien Yang's reference to volunteer work, forming relationships with people in activities in which you have a chance to see their character can only help shed light on their trustworthiness early on. "There are usually signs, serendipitous signs," Reinemund said when I asked how you can ascertain a person's true character. "You see them at church one day or they're out doing volunteer work. Or maybe there's a comment made in a meeting that really gets at the fundamental underpinnings of how the person thinks, rather than just an articulation of an analysis in a P and L."

Don't Overdo It

Your career is a marathon, not a sprint, so try to pace yourself. John Swainson cautioned me that some people take on too much. "I think you can go overboard, and spend an enormous amount of time networking as a CEO. I try to balance that," he told me. "In fact, I've cut back a lot of the things I did when I was a new CEO because, frankly, I don't have time for them and I'm not sure they're the best use of my time. And there are people who I know who come to every business roundtable and every conceivable meeting known to man, and I've just had to ultimately say, 'No, I can't possibly do that.' And I don't." Set your own limits, and treat networking like any task on your calendar—analyze its helpfulness and how much of your time it's worth.

People network everywhere and anywhere, and where you choose to do it will also become part of your personal style. "To me, networking is part of working," Russ Fradin told me. "I don't go to cocktail parties. It's just not something I enjoy. I don't play golf." And while others let hobbies or sports double as networking opportunities, to him they're better left separate. He just prefers to find the best player out there. "I play tennis at a very competitive level, and most of the people I've played, if you told them I was a CEO, you'd probably knock them over with a feather. They have no idea."

And, of course, others were distinctly cool about the idea. "I would say I'm not a huge networker," Todd Stitzer told me. "I think some networking and some intelligence about what's going on in the outer world or in the world outside of your company is a good thing, but too much of it is energy sapping and distracting. It's a wonderful concept, but I've rarely found time to actually employ it the way it's been described."

Again, the amount of time and the importance you place on networking is completely up to you. "I think it's a matter of time," Steve Reinemund told me. "How much time does the individual have and what's the motive for doing it? In the course of some jobs you have more exposure to the outside world than others, and being able to learn from others outside in that environment is great. To seek out people in that community for the purpose of creating a broader network or options in the future, one has to think about [whether] it's a good use of your time versus being at home with your kids at night, or being able to put another hour into doing something productive at work. It's all a matter of priorities and time."

With A Strong Network, You're Never Alone

With all the talk of emotional deposits and returning favors, remember finally that a strong network works double duty as a support system. Many of the executives referred to their support system when I asked them about some of the frustrations and challenges of the job, so much so that it became clear to me that although on the surface "networking" brings to mind finding jobs and making business deals, ultimately it's the foundation of people who can help you with the day-to-day. "I don't think [being a CEO] is a lonely job, because in all circumstances I have been able to find people and colleagues to share the burden," Lucas Chow told me. "I am very fortunate that

I've been able to find like-minded colleagues who share the same kind of passion. These are the people that most probably appreciate the pain and suffering that I have been through."

To Bill Swanson it's all about family. "There are people who are amazed that I'll get to know them," he told me. "And somebody will have a problem, and I'll say, 'Well, do you know so-and-so, let me call them for you.' My friends know that it's kind of the way I grew up in a European household. You came to our house, you always got fed. You always had something to drink. You were always welcome. The door was open, and it's that way today. For me, anybody around me knows that [they've] got an open invite. I always say nobody likes a grump but another grump. And people want to be around people who can help them. When you have crises in life or in business, you find out really soon who your friends are. That's when you have this real core network that you depend on that people will come and rally for you, and there's usually some in there you never expected."

Executive Summary

You are already part of a network. Though executives differ on how much value they think there is in networking, all concede that it is going on all the time and you might as well approach it rationally and get the best from it. In fact it is happening when you don't even know it, and some people's careers can be changed dramatically because somebody told somebody else something about them. But remember, it's not about getting someone to recommend you for a job. It's a two-way support system.

Networking begins at home. Often executives can lose touch with what's happening and being talked about in remote corners of their companies, and networking within the company—seeing certain in-touch individuals on a regular basis—can help overcome this.

Emotional deposits. Networking is like many other forms of social life—it involves giving and taking, but not always at the same time. When you do something for someone, you make an emotional deposit on which you might draw in the future. It is part of the bonding that goes on in the business community.

Less lonely at the top. Having good connections outside the company can provide opportunities for executives to exchange ideas and compare notes with like-minded businessmen who have similar problems and solutions. It's not about sharing corporate secrets, but sharing personal perspectives. And you can also enjoy the social and sporting side while you are about it. But don't let it become yet another thing to steal time away from your family and attention to your health.

Someone older and wiser. Networks are often the means by which budding chief executives develop mentors. Not everyone thinks a mentor is a good thing, and some warn that some people act as mentors in their own interests. But the right person, with the right experience and attitude, and who has been there and done that, can help you see things in ways you would not otherwise have done.

Chapter 5

Getting the Message Across

As the founder and chairman of Biocon, Asia's largest biotechnology firm, Kiran Mazumdar-Shaw is one of India's most powerful women. But one of her priorities at her company is to make sure everyone calls her by her first name. "Everyone calls me Kiran," she told me proudly when we met in Bangalore. "In India we have a very hierarchical reporting system, but I said the first thing in Biocon we should learn to do is call each other by our first names."

Kiran Mazumdar-Shaw (she is married to a Scot, John Shaw), now in her mid-fifties, is India's richest woman, referred to as "India's Biotech Queen" by *The Economist* and "India's mother of invention" by *The New York Times.* An honors degree graduate in zoology from Bangalore University, she decided to turn entrepreneur and use her microbiological training to start Biocon India Ltd. at age twenty-five.

A first-name basis is part of Mazumdar-Shaw's strategy in building her corporate culture. "I am hell-bent on a flat organization, a very interactive organization," she told me. "I don't like there to be this thing of 'Oh, you will have to talk to my boss first, I can't talk directly to you.' It's not just in India; I find this in big companies a lot, where they are so territorial and concerned about status and titles and how you report to each other. It's acute, even in American companies."

There isn't an executive anywhere who hasn't stressed communication as a vital part of their role. For Mazumdar-Shaw, the no-last-name policy is just the start, and every CEO has his or her own method. Russ Fradin of Hewitt, for example, launched a CEO blog. When I asked him what would happen if an employee made a negative comment in response to a post, he reassured me that there are no negative consequences. And, in fact, that day he was planning to blog on the very topic of establishing an environment in which people are not afraid to speak up. Bill Swanson of Raytheon makes sure that at the end of each day he goes to bed with a "clean screen," which means he responds to each e-mail that lands in his in-box. "Everybody knows my e-mail address, and I answer every one of them," he told me. Through the writing of this book, I found that to be absolutely true.

Astonishingly, Ben Verwaayen of BT Group also said he answered all his e-mails—and he was talking about ones from customers. I never tested him on this, but a reporter from the British newspaper *The Guardian* once did. After an interview with him, the reporter sent Verwaayen an e-mail. Three minutes later, the reporter said, Verwaayen replied: "Yes, I do answer all emails myself and I get hundreds a week."

Good, clear, and frequent communication is an essential part of running a company today, whether it is to convey news (good and bad) to employees, keep people in the loop, show staffers that their bosses are human beings with a heart, or convey feedback about the business from those staffers to those bosses. That does not mean there is a formula you can follow: good communication needs to be in keeping with other aspects of an executive's character, not grafted on. But there are some essential elements of good communication that you can learn and refine. Only the style is your own.

"I don't think it's impossible to teach yourself the appropriate means of communication that are effective for you as an individual leader," Todd Stitzer of Cadbury Schweppes told me. "But leadership without communication is impossible. Some people are shy and reserved, and other people are more voluble. But if you are a thoughtful business leader, you have to recognize that the people who are on your team seek and need communication about the [company's] objectives. They want to know how progress is being made on the objectives. They want to celebrate if the objectives are met. If you are not sensitive to that dynamic, I think it would be difficult for you to be a successful leader." In short, he summed up: "You pick the style, you pick the moment, you pick the medium, but you need to do it."

Much of what that is about is clarity. Make those objectives clear, couched in plain language that everyone who works for you can understand. Everyone in an organization should be aware of the company's accomplishments and current goals. Rick Dreiling told me what it was like when he took over at Duane Reade. "When we got here, I remember looking at everybody and saying . . . 'Who are we, what are we?' and nobody could give me the answer. And I am not a mission statement guy. I never, ever, ever believed in mission statements. . . . I am a guy who is all about, 'You got to have a plan that can be executed.' It has to be incredibly simple, and you just feed on that plan and feed on it. So, we took—I hate to say I called it a mission statement and a value statement—but what we did was we just articulated it into just a couple of bullet points and we talk about those things constantly."

I asked each of the executives I interviewed to communicate to me, as it were, the ways they talk to their people and they talk back. Everyone I spoke with emphasized the staggering importance of open—and honest—interaction with their staffs.

Good Communication = Great Leadership

Rick Dreiling described why good communication is crucial, even more so than having the magnetic personality one might assume a CEO needs. "Great CEOs do not have to be charismatic, but they have the ability to have such clarity in the way they speak, that people sign up and they follow," he said. "And they have the ability to articulate how people are doing on the journey. They have the time to provide feedback. I think also, if you think about great CEOs, they have the ability to make you feel like you are the most important person on the earth when they are talking to you." Indeed, look at the examples around you. Whom do you admire for the way they convey information and treat the people around them? Who makes a mess of it, and why? These are your firsthand case studies. Take notes.

It's more than a matter of style and grace. Long gone are the days when patrician managers ran their companies with the paternalistic manners they learned from an elite upbringing. Now what matters is what works. We know that shouting until you're blue in the face doesn't work, but neither is it enough to say clearly what you want done. What matters is your ability to inspire effective action through your words.

In spite of, or perhaps he would say *because of,* his experience in the U.S. Army (he is a graduate of the U.S. Military Academy at West Point and has an MBA from Harvard), JCPenney's Kenneth Hicks believes in getting the message across much less directly than barking orders. His head of marketing often accompanies him on the frequent visits he makes to stores and, said Hicks, once made this observation: "'You know, Ken, you very, very seldom ever tell somebody, "Just do this." What you do is you ask questions until the person says, yeah, and the light comes on.'" Hicks told him, "The reason I do that is because if I tell you to move this bottle from here to here, or from here to here, you'd say, 'Okay, fine. Ken told me to move the bottle from here to here, so I did.'" But by asking employees questions about their work, he helps people to understand for themselves, for example, that "there's a better place to put the bottle so it doesn't get in the way when you get the glass." When employees come up with a solution on their own, they'll actually understand why it's a good idea. Hicks is a big man, military in every way in his bearing, in the way he speaks, and in the way he defines leadership, and proud of all those things. But he is not intimidating.

Perhaps Hicks is the kind of man Nadia Zaal, CEO of Al Barari, had in mind when she suggested good communicators were born, not made: "I'm going to say something a little bit controversial because, of course, you can develop skills, but I just think that people skills are something that you either . . . have or you don't."

Bill Amelio related an amusing anecdote that perfectly illustrated how *not* to communicate. He told me of an incident involving an executive from another company at a volunteer event, which he said is one of the best places to see true leadership skills (or the lack thereof) in action. "This executive had a passion for a particular project that would take several days. The first day of the project, he probably had fifteen people with him. He was pushing hard trying to get things done but he was not treating his team well. The second day, I noticed he had only half the people there. By the fourth day, he was by himself. People chose not to stay. They chose to be somewhere else. Once you realize—especially in a philanthropic endeavor—that people have a choice, you also realize that you have to lead well, treat people well and demonstrate respect and gratitude, or people will leave you there alone. The moral is to treat all your people as if they are volunteers."

To be sure, people notice and talk about poor communication—and good communication—because it is so visible, which is something Arthur Collins of Medtronic observed. "One thing that certainly became a larger part of the [CEO] role than . . . it was a long time ago was the importance of communication and the degree to which [people] watch [executives] very closely and listen very carefully to what they say or what they do," he said. "I had an individual tell me when I first became a vice president at Abbott Laboratories, 'You're going to be very surprised at how much people will watch what you do and listen to what you say. They'll take away much more than you think should be taken away from your words, little words, or little things that you do.'"

Those "little" things, for many of the CEOs I spoke to, start with basic niceties that we take for granted. They told me that they let their employees know they care, in however small a way, by sending cards or remembering something personal about them. "Show that you're accessible and that you want to be approached and that you care about people," Russ Fradin said. "It's showing [that] everybody's important."

Of course, if you're the head of a large company, being accessible to all your employees takes much more effort, and the CEOs I spoke to proved themselves up to the task. "When I ran our plant in Andover, we had seven thousand people," Bill Swanson of Raytheon told me. "Two-thirds of the people I knew by name. And I knew something about the families of at least fifty percent of the people in the plant. I walked the floor every day."

Kiran Mazumdar-Shaw knows it's impossible to remember everyone by name. "I used to know everyone by name when we were at least five hundred people," she told me. "Today we are three thousand people so I don't know everybody by name, and I just have to smile at people. When I interact with people I try to give the impression . . . that I'm just an ordinary person." Well, ordinary enough. When I visited her offices, she was dressed in an elegant salwar kameez, a traditional two-piece north Indian garment, and was personable and casual, though full of energy and focus.

Don't Just Hear What's Been Said: Listen

Listening comes in a variety of forms. Martin Homlish of SAP demonstrated the more formal one in an earlier chapter.

Homlish feels that the follow-up to a conversation is even more important than the conversation itself. The worst thing that you can do is to have grand listening sessions, get all the problems on the table, and then not act on them. Sometimes, acting on them means that you go back to the individual and say that while you've heard the problem, you are not going to change it because there are other issues that are affected by it.

"So," Homlish concluded, "it's about small victories and it's about communicating those small victories."

Kiran Mazumdar-Shaw thrives on listening to opinions that may not seem popular. "I have always encouraged people to speak their minds," she told me. And that policy has its effects. "Sometimes, some of my colleagues who are very outspoken and vociferous come in and don't agree with certain things that we are discussing. We get into very animated debates, and then somebody is wondering whether the guy who has had this talk with me is going to get the sack. And I say, 'Oh, that's just a normal discussion we are having.' "

So brace yourself, especially if you really want to open the floodgates the way Ben Verwaayen did when he went in front of his company and said, "You know, guys, I'm going to make a plea to you. I'm going to remove the biggest barrier that you have in front of you. Tell me what it is." Then someone stood up and told Verwaayen, "The biggest barrier is you. If I have an idea I go to my boss, and my boss goes to his boss, and she goes to you, and if it doesn't fit in your head, you will say, 'Hmm, I don't think so.' So my idea is dead. So at the end of the day this company cannot outgrow the size of your head."

Instead of getting angry, Verwaayen said, "You're actually right.

You're one hundred percent right." Today, the employee is still with the company. "The art of letting go is, I think, the most important thing to inspire other people," Verwaayen told me in retrospect. "And [that was a] defining moment. I think you get the opportunity in your career to have defining moments, and the ability to have a story like this."

If that seemed a generous response to a difficult situation, Verwaayen's attitude did not surprise me. His generosity was evident right from the beginning of the interview. Due to a delayed flight, I had to race from Gatwick to my hotel and made it to our appointment at BT Group in central London with just minutes to spare. Verwaayen was quick to set me at ease. "Relax," he told me. "We've all been there."

Being open to feedback can allow you to bring about positive changes, but before you open up the channels, think hard about how you're going to take it all in. Carl Bass of Autodesk was also brutally frank on this topic. "When most people say they're open to change, they're full of crap," he said. Then he laid it on the line, saying that if I asked the staffs of the CEOs I interviewed for this book whether their boss is truly open to change, "maybe half would say that their boss is really open to change and to feedback." Then, he conceded, "That may be said of me, too, but I think it's something to aspire to, and we absolutely should. If nothing else, if you don't understand the effect [you have] on the people around you, it's very hard to know how to motivate and lead people."

Physical Environment Counts

Part of showing your employees that you're human and approachable is creating a work environment where people can feel comfortable.

Nadia Zaal expects the best from her staff, but she also makes sure she relaxes with them and gives them space to let go, even at work. "We have a routine now where at ten in the morning and four in the afternoon, we gather in the kitchen and we have a corporate chef that cooks healthy food for everyone," she said. "We all gather and generally mingle and chat. No shoptalk is allowed."

Zaal also encourages people to have meetings in the less-formal setting of the rooftop garden at the company's Dubai headquarters. She also installed a treadmill in the office in case people need to blow off steam. "I encourage them to take lots of breaks throughout the day." She makes sure the conversation is varied. "I always make sure I spend time talking to different people within the company, but not all about work," she told me. "So I think I have a good personal connection with the staff."

Kiran Mazumdar-Shaw also found that a hierarchy-free eating area is a great equalizer. She doesn't like the idea of exclusive dining rooms, so she did away with it. "We have a normal canteen where all of us eat, from day one," she told me. "I know this is not really the normal set way of doing things. And even if we get VIP visitors, we take them to the canteen. Why should we separate ourselves? Why should we say that we are the chosen few, and select few, who can sit in a very fancy dining room?" She hopes her behavior helps increase morale overall. Her employees know she has to put up with what everyone else does, even standing in line for food. "When people come and tell me, 'Ma'am, come in, sit down,' when they see me standing, I say, 'Look, if there is a queue, I have to wait just like you guys have to wait.' And of course they say, 'Are you sure you're sure?' So then they don't complain so much."

Bob Reynolds of Fidelity gave an example of someone he worked with at NCNB (now Bank of America), Hugh McColl. "I didn't work directly for him but we were very, very close and I thought he was the greatest leader I have seen," Reynolds recalled fondly. "He would do things like on Friday afternoon, he'd go down to the credit department, which was all your young MBAs, and say, 'Come on. We're going drinking.' And he'd take them to the place next to the bank and he'd sit there for an hour or two and tell stories. He was part of the team and he made everyone feel like, 'Hey, the head of the organization cares about us.' He had a public persona but his persona inside the organization was totally not that."

Russ Fradin finds that remembering the little things goes a long way. One of his staffers mentioned he was training for his first marathon, so Fradin dropped him a note asking how it went after he was done. Chatting with another employee, he discovered he was planning a trek in the Himalayas. "When he got back I wrote him a little note and said, 'How'd you survive the thin air?'" he told me when we met in Chicago. "Just the fact that you remember something and ask something they didn't expect has an effect on people." It sounds rather simple—and it is—yet in a given day it's easy to get caught up with the business. Navigating the duties of a C-suiter is multifaceted— while much of it is operational and technical, the softer side of managing just comes down to making small talk and remembering the little details. For the most successful CEOs, these qualities come naturally, but even they have to remind themselves.

Title Doesn't Matter

Walt Bettinger of Charles Schwab told me a story he said he'll never forget. As an undergraduate at Ohio University, he took an evening class in strategy during his last quarter of senior year. "It met from seven to ten at night, and we were getting close to graduating, feeling pretty good about ourselves . . . we're going to change the world and be all these big things. It came down to the final exam and the professor handed [it] out . . . it was just a single [blank] piece of paper. . . . He said, 'Your final exam is one question. You're all smart, you're all going to go out and change the world and achieve all these things, accomplish all this kind of stuff. You know all I can teach you about business. Your final exam is: for three hours a night, twice a week for the last ten weeks you've been in this building; we've taken breaks—we always took one or two breaks each session. What's the name of the lady who cleans the building?'

"I didn't know Dottie's name that night, but I've tried to know every Dottie since," Bettinger told me. "It was powerful, because we'd gone through all these hours and all this strategy and case studies, but that was the lesson that stayed. Knowing and appreciating and linking to people is so powerful."

Today Bill Swanson could be teaching the class Bettinger took, because he said nearly the same thing to me. "I tell people that if you don't know the name of the person who serves you your lunch or cleans your office, you ought to question something. And that is yourself." It's a philosophy he practices, making sure he knows the name of the server when he goes out to dinner (and has a conversation with him or her).

In his characteristically matter-of-fact way, Joseph Lawler of CMGI brushed aside questions of hierarchy, acknowledging on the one hand that there is one, while on the other hand maintaining that it doesn't matter. "Those who are in charge don't really need to act like they're in charge. Everybody knows they're in charge. So the hierarchy, which is so egocentric . . . get over it. That's not really the way businesses work today."

Terrance Marks of Coca-Cola told me, "The best leaders that I've met are the people who are equally comfortable walking through a warehouse talking to a loader or walking into a CEO suite for a meeting with a customer."

Keep People in the Loop

No one wants to feel overlooked and left out, and that is especially true of your employees. Even if there's nothing to say, say something. This, in essence, is what John Kealey of iDirect told me. "Sometimes you need to communicate even if there's nothing to communicate, because that in and of itself helps update people," he said. "As an example, when we signed the deal to sell the company to Singapore Technologies, every Monday morning I gave the team an update on what was happening relative to closing the deal. Even if there was nothing to update. Even if it was, 'Guys, the update today is nothing material happened last week.'" To Kealey, making the effort to send out the no-news memo is important. "What I'm trading off with them is the agreement that if I update you every Monday morning, you guys won't spend time talking about it during the week. There is no value in that. But I just update them every week." When I met with Kealey in the summer of 2007, he had an even more salient example. He was about to step down as CEO, but he didn't keep his team in the dark. "I've been updating them regularly on here's what's going on in the search," he told me. "'Here's who's going to make the decision, here are the candidates, what kind of candidates we're looking at.' I couldn't share names because of confidentiality but I updated them all the time on that."

Kealey demonstrates that it's worth making that extra effort, as he did when he came to meet me personally at reception and walked me back to his office for the interview.

Indeed, Hicks believes you can never "overcommunicate." "At the senior level there are some people who are very proud of the fact, 'Well, I don't do e-mail, or I don't like voice mail.' You have to take advantage of all the means of communication that you have. And we communicate with people frequently and repeatedly. Our strategy, we're constantly talking about the elements of our strategy to the people, all the time. We figure after about two hundred times, they probably will have it down. So if you haven't heard it a couple hundred times, then we probably haven't done it enough."

Creating an Open Culture Worldwide

Having solid communication in your company, from social niceties to official memos, is crucial today especially in light of the broadening global landscape. Nandan Nilekani of Infosys Technologies explained this to me in the context of globalization. He tries to "create an environment where there is a much freer flow of ideas: as we become more of a fluid, global, network organization, the role of corporate headquarters diminishes," he said, echoing the thoughts of several other CEOs (see chapter 6). Because he and his staffers are more spread out and constantly on the road, communication is that much more important. But it works, he said, "as long as you have high communication among the senior leadership, because there's a part of our organization which is still central. Your human resources practices, your values, your legal analytical behavior, your financial reporting. All these things still have to adhere to some global standards. You still need someone to drive these kind of things."

But with employees on opposite ends of the globe, how do you maintain some kind of communication hub? Aside from jumping on planes yourself, the answer is: embrace technology. Learn it, use it, make it work for you. Bill Swanson, who, as we know, makes sure every e-mail in his in-box is taken care of before he completes his day, said that anyone aspiring to fill his shoes needs to be able to handle the same kinds of e-mails he gets, whether they're from disgruntled employees or not. "My advice is to be very comfortable with communication. Communication not only down, but sideways and up," he argued. "And they should be very comfortable with brevity—nothing drives a senior person more up a wall than getting a two-page e-mail, and you have to read the whole thing to get to the punch line." Remember, too, that e-mails are easily misconstrued, which makes it even more worth your while to learn to craft effective, brief e-mails. You're going to be getting a lot of them!

Swanson felt that today's and especially tomorrow's CEOs are going to have to be more comfortable communicating with entry-level employees. With social networking and e-mail, the current generation has no qualms about expressing their opinion through a digital interface. Your decision making does not change. Only your mode of communication does. Obviously the feedback to an entry-level employee is going to be very different from that you would give a senior executive.

Kenneth Hicks stressed the need to be a little old-fashioned sometimes, even in a world of advanced communications: "I do use e-mail," he said. "At the same time, at the end of every month, [for] all the buyers who beat their plan in sales and profit for the month and the stores, I hand-sign a personal letter to them."

Jim Donald, former CEO of Starbucks, said, "Two or three times a month I would send a personal note to the spouses and the kids of my executives saying, 'Thanks for letting me borrow Sarah. I know she's been traveling a lot, but it's been very important to the company. I hope you're well. Let me know if I can do anything for you, Billy, and Joe. Signed, Jim Donald, CEO.'" It was gestures like that which inspired loyalty from his executives' families. "You know what the husband would say? 'Thanks for reaching out and talking to me about this. No one's ever done that to me before.'"

An e-mail is devoid of emotion. Therefore, you should avoid heated discussion or defensive feedback through this medium. Even a phone call or a limited conference call is better than e-mail in this regard.

Give and Ask for Feedback

An open-communication policy has its inevitable consequences. As soon as you open up the channels, the "communication" we've been talking about will start coming your way, like it or not. Russ Fradin, for example, told me that employees will come up to him in the dining room with a problem, expecting him to solve it then and there.

Some things that people tell you will be unexpected, but take it in your stride. I asked Nadia Zaal about feedback that has surprised her, and she told me, "I've learned a lot about myself on this job, and the one thing that surprises me which I still don't understand is that I tend to think of myself as being friendly with everyone and I try to be as informal as possible, but people would say, 'Oh, but you're intimidating' or 'You're very forceful.'"

Bob Reynolds of Fidelity has his own special approach, but be very careful about trying to emulate it. Get it wrong and it can have the opposite effect of what you intended. People have to get to know his style, he said. "You know, some people go, 'Boy, Bob's really giving me a hard time about the advertising [for example].' You know, I would say, 'Obviously we don't want to sell anything this quarter, right? I mean, from the ads.'" His sarcasm can be misconstrued, but his employees know to expect it from him. He knows people at his company tell each other, "If he's not giving you a hard time, he doesn't like you. If he was pissed he would just say, 'You're out.'"

Reynolds gave another example: "If I think [something] is going too slow in its development I'll say, 'Well, it looks like I'm gonna be an old man before you get [this thing] up and running. Do I have to come down [there] and [do it] myself, and why?'"

I asked Reynolds if he recommended this caustic approach to others. At first he agreed that it helped build relationships, but then he warned that it could backfire. "There was a guy who worked for me, and he and I could say the exact same thing to the same person. They would be pissed at him and love me. The way he did it was like he meant it."

Even if you are good at the one-liner or the affectionate put-down, be careful where you practice it. It doesn't always travel. Raimundo Morales, formerly of Peru's Banco de Crédito, wasn't commenting specifically on the Reynolds method when I asked him about executive communications style in Latin America, but he observed that overall "we're perhaps a little bit less direct in transmitting our thoughts and our feelings than they would be in the U.S." He called it "a little bit more political," by which he said he meant less "frontal" or "aggressive."

Arthur Collins, at the end of his interview, reiterated something he had said several times and that echoed Ken Hicks's view that you can never overcommunicate: "Effectively communicate, communicate, communicate." He added, "I would underscore, most people think that's you communicating orally or in a written manner. I think the lost art of communications is listening—it's a lost art, especially the more successful you get. The real good leaders understand the importance of listening and asking questions as opposed to just telling people what to do."

Communicating with Customers

Many of the comments I received on marketing to customers were surprising. I was not told that what matters can be measured on a scorecard—by the amount of brand exposure or the number of press mentions and promotional events. For Martin Homlish, SAP's chief marketing officer, everything points toward one thing—telling it like it really is. "You have to truly understand the DNA of the company that you are marketing. You have to truly understand what makes that company successful. You have to understand the culture. You have to understand the people. You have to understand the product, the customers. Then you have to be able to translate all of that into a visual language, into an audible language and into a style and a tone and a brand promise that ultimately reflects all of those characteristics. Because the key about good advertising and branding . . . is truth telling."

One of the most important functions of a chief executive is to be the custodian of the best customers of the company. While they are most likely serviced by your top client relationship executives, customers love to know that they are important to you. Bill Nuti cut short our conversation by saying, "Look, I'm really enjoying this conversation and we can continue later, but one of my top customers is on the phone and I have to take the call." The best executives will drop everything but the most crucial matters to take a client call whether they are calling with good or bad news. They are also credible with the clients because of a reputation honed over time by being responsive and truthful.

Honesty Is the Best Policy

No matter how accomplished you might be as a communicator of good news, the time is bound to come when you have to give the bad. "Twenty years ago, it took a while for bad information to get out, but today we're in an instant communication age," Bill Swanson told me. "Bad news travels in a nanosecond. You have to be able to deal with it internally, externally, and sometimes globally. So you've got to be very comfortable dealing with that, knowing you're going to have to manage it."

Swanson and everyone else who had a view on it said, above all, be honest. "Being honest and direct with people pays dividends," Russ

Fradin said. Todd Stitzer told me that when he counsels rising C-suiters, "I always advise them that bad news is better soon rather than later. If there is bad news, people should own up to it completely, transparently." That said, he continued, the best way to deal with it is to immediately offer solutions. "They should not dramatically offer to fall on their sword," Stitzer said. "They should seek to describe the situation, describe the causes, and most importantly, suggest a solution. Pointing the finger at some other cause or reason that doesn't ring true is not a good thing to do. Accept responsibility, describe the situation, and describe the solution."

As a CFO, Steven Crane of CMGI knows about communicating bad news. "First of all, you've got to get all the facts. One thing I've found is, don't just react and go running in and say we've got an issue. Because the CEO is going to come up with five questions. What I have to do is anticipate those five questions and get them answered before I walk through that door."

I asked Ben Verwaayen straight out how he communicates the worst news of all: you're fired. "With respect," Verwaayen said. "It's not a power struggle. Why would I break a person's inner confidence and say, 'You're no good at all'? If it's a performance issue, well, it is in the eye of the beholder. It is [a matter of] time, place, and circumstances. So yes, it may be a performance issue here but maybe not in the next spot you're in. Maybe this was just not for you. That's not what I do. I [would] say, 'John, it doesn't work. Could be me, could be you, but it doesn't work.'" Verwaayen told me he would then turn the situation into an opportunity to give the person perspective. "For many people [that] is a kind of liberation. They get an opportunity to rethink where they are. I've helped many people to the next step. In some cases it's just [that] the personalities didn't work. I happen to be in this chair, you're in that chair, bad luck and so we have to do something. I still have respect for you." In this case, communication isn't just a way with words, but an underlying regard for the people you're dealing with. In short, communicating well is having compassion.

Arthur Collins maintained that the idea that honesty is the best policy comes from the fact that people are not that easily fooled. "It is very difficult, and it doesn't make any sense, to take a course of action and not be truthful and not tell it like it is to employees. They're smart. Most people can deal very well with the facts, but they don't deal very well with uncertainty. So, as quickly as you can, lay out both the opportunities, the challenges, and what we're going to do about it, and not have indecision and uncertainty rule. That just drives people up the wall. You can deal with a bad set of conditions if you know what they are."

To be "on brand," as he put it, is to be truthful. "You need to look at everything. It's not just the big picture. It's not just the advertising and the events that you run, but it's everything from the business cards, to the music you play on hold, to the way a telephone is answered, to the quality of the writing of correspondence back and forth to customers.

"Everything that you do that touches the customer has an impact on either making a positive deposit in the brand equity bank or making a withdrawal."

Executive Summary

Make yourself human. Talk to people, know their names and what they do, and show a genuine interest in their lives. There are some principles of communication you can learn, so watch those around you as you move up the ranks, but find a style that is really you, and remember it doesn't go down the same way in every culture.

Are you listening? It's not just an art—it's a must. When you say you want feedback, take it and do something with it. Employees hate phony conversations with their bosses.

Let there be life. Create places and times for people to talk and relax and feel like they belong. Eat in the canteen and stand in line like everybody else.

Ignore the rankings. Forget about titles and hierarchies—people know who the boss is and who has the final say.

Don't leave people guessing. Say what's going on when everybody knows something important is being decided—even when there's nothing new to tell. There is no such thing as overcommunicating.

Be tech-savvy, not tech-obsessed. Technology makes it possible for us to talk directly to one another, from the bottom of the company to the top and from one end of the world to the next. Use it, but don't abuse it.

Tell the truth. Even when the news is bad—especially when the news is bad—be good at saying what you have to say, and that's the truth.

Chapter 6

A World of Opportunity

The nineteenth-century journalist Horace Greeley said, "Go west, young man" in reference to the burgeoning frontier. But when I met with Sanjiv Ahuja of Orange and asked him what advice he would give up-and-coming C-suiters, he turned that old saying on its head. "I would say, 'Go east, young man,' " he said. Ahuja, who is from India but is based in London and has worked in the United States, is well positioned to understand the importance of going global. Having global experience is becoming a prerequisite for today's CEO. You should have experience dealing with multiple cultures, foreign customers, and a distributed workforce.

Regardless of the size, industry, or home base of their companies, executives I spoke to agreed that globalization is not just a buzzword. As Bill Nuti of NCR put it unambiguously, "If you are a CEO without global experience, I think you're doing the job with one hand tied behind your back."

Just as important as any of the strategies and skills that C-suiters discuss in these pages, the ability to position yourself globally, both individually and as a representative of your company, is crucial. "[If] you're in some utility industry where all you do is give power to

Southern California, it's okay, but if you're going to be running Procter and Gamble or GE or Goldman Sachs, you need to have global exposure," Nandan Nilekani of Infosys Technologies told me. "If you want to be successful in the C-suite in India, or you want to be successful in the C-suite in the West, those managers with a global footprint in their backgrounds are definitely much better placed."

Obviously, working abroad is your surest way of getting global experience, but you can also start by drawing upon and optimizing your own background. John Swainson of CA, Inc., for example, recognizes what he learned from growing up in Canada, and from his experience at IBM. "I certainly wouldn't claim that Canada is global or diverse, but it at least gave me a perspective for what it was like to operate outside the U.S., and the kinds of challenges people had," he told me. "And I must say, IBM was very attuned to the global perspective. I think that even that is not going to be sufficient, though, in the future." He believes that what you need now to move up the ladder to general manager will have to include expertise gained abroad.

Javier Gutiérrez, president of Ecopetrol, Colombia's largest company, pointed out that to be an ambitious executive in a smaller Latin American country such as his can mean you operate in a more competitive environment, quite simply because there are fewer companies. "On the other hand," he said, "economical and political conditions in the region create an environment of uncertainty." The institutional and legal frameworks can also be extremely complex. All of which means business is harder, requiring a higher investment of time in risk analysis, since forecasts are difficult to make. On a positive note, such difficulties "contribute to the development of good skills, creativity, innovation, and resourcefulness," said Gutiérrez.

In addition to its home base of Colombia, Ecopetrol has operations in Peru, Bolivia, Ecuador, Brazil, and Central America. This has meant that Gutiérrez and his team have had to develop the ability to relate to cultures and people from different countries and to be able to adapt to different environments. "This strength helps generate confidence to achieve good business deals. It's essential to learn to connect with others," he said.

When Ahuja said "go east," he meant India and China, of course, and those are the two countries emphasized by every other CEO I spoke with. "You need to have an understanding of what's going on in India and China and the dynamic there," Swainson said. "Then you need to have an understanding of the differences in the way people use our products around the world. Even though we have a product line that is more or less the same everywhere, the dynamic of how it's used is very different, and if you don't understand the underlying causes for that, you can spend a lot of time and a lot of money—and get it wrong."

That said, do not be daunted by the big wide world. François Barrault of BT Global Services does what many of the CEOs whom I've spoken to do—he approaches something that might seem intimidating and finds a new way of looking at it. "You can use the planet as a playground," he said, especially when your product or service is evolving and innovative. As with all other aspects of high-level management, seen as a challenge and an opportunity, globalization can shake up the way you look at almost anything, even when it is not directly related to geography.

I specifically sought out CEOs from around the world, a number of them in India and other parts of Asia, who could offer their insights for this book, but no matter where a CEO was based, even in an American company, they all offered invaluable advice for establishing your own "global footprint," as Nilekani called it.

Get Out Your Passport

Bill Amelio of Lenovo has lived in Singapore for seven years. "Before I moved here, I would have thought a company could survive without focusing on cultural diversity. The reality is companies can survive that way. But they are ultimately limited. Working overseas, you get a totally different view. A place like Singapore is a great cultural melting pot. You have a fantastic opportunity to experience so many different cultures—different nationalities, religions, and perspectives coming together in one unique place." Amelio advocates learning about diversity firsthand early on, and to be open to it. "A key learning for me has been this: companies have to look deeper into the value of diversity. Corporations must embrace diversity as a source of strength to tackle the global market."

Not only is it a strength to understand it, but it'll help you make more informed decisions as a manager and member of the C-suite. "The way I operate is, I go to where the stuff is, where the action is," Barrault, a French national, told me. "Because if you go to India, if you go to Bangalore or Brazil or Shanghai or Danyang in China, you see the people." He then described some on-location experiences that helped him understand what it was like to actually be there. "Everybody was talking about China without having been to China; people were talking about globalization without staying overseas. I went to Danyang, which nobody knows. Maybe it is thought to be a little bit dead. I met the mayor of Danyang, then I went to the university [there] and I saw twelve thousand students learning ICT [information and communications technology]. I saw a huge open space with hundreds and hundreds of students who were all entrepreneurs. They were dealing with the next-generation, most advanced technology. I remember when I came into this huge room I saw that and I had a big flash [of insight]." Barrault got to know a vital, cutting-edge place that had been thought sleepy and unknown, but he wouldn't have had any idea of it had he not visited. He had a similar experience in India. "If you don't go there, talk to the students, look how the people are, you don't get it," he said.

Steve Reinemund of PepsiCo acknowledged that his successor, Indra Nooyi, who is Indian, brought more global experience to the job than he did. "Her international perspective was clearly broader than mine," he said. "I acquired some over time with the job, but that was a large part of a strong portfolio to become CEO. She had worldwide perspective. And it's not just a matter of learning. It's a matter of thinking broadly, thinking on a global basis, which, because of her background, [is] just the way she thought. And that's critical for a CEO, particularly for a company like ours where most of our growth is going to come internationally."

Ron Williams of Aetna said, "I encourage people to get global international experience early. It's extremely important. I also encourage people to have multiple language skills, which I don't have. I'm still working on English here! If I were speaking to a young executive, I would say that I think international experience is important and language skills are important."

While living and working abroad has many advantages, it can take its toll on you personally because you need more private resources than you do at home. When you live at home, for instance, you have friends and family to take care of the kids in an emergency or to call if you have a medical problem. That's when family really matters, according to Arthur Collins, CEO of Medtronic: "If you have a strong family unit, it gets stronger because you have to rely very much on yourselves for much of what has been available to you in the community that you come from. If you don't have a strong family, it will really show the cracks quickly."

Get Ready

I asked a number of executives how young managers can prepare themselves for this changing corporate world. The answer was to take advantage of the fact that companies are looking to cultivate employees who can help with their global expansion. So if you've got the languages and the drive, go in search of an assignment abroad or, if you can't go abroad, look for a job managing international divisions from your home base.

I asked John Kealey of iDirect if he'd take an employee out of Akron, Ohio, for example, and give him global experience, and he said it would be trial by fire, but he's willing to do it. As an example, he said his VP of sales for the Americas just took a position handling all global sales. "He's in Denver, Colorado, and he's never really sold outside the Americas, and the big part for him is, 'Let's go, let's get out there, let's see what it's like,'" Kealey told me. When you get that assignment, do not be intimidated: remember that in many ways it's just a matter of doing your job. "You can focus on the differences in the international markets, and that's important, but I think it's also important to focus on the similarities," Kealey said. "For us, we sell to other businesses. We're a business-to-business company. What do all businesses want to do? They want to make money. They have customers they want to support, so [you have to] understand what value proposition they have. It's the same as you do in the U.S. Then you overlay on that some of the cultural differences, [perhaps] in the way somebody likes to meet, or the way they like to negotiate."

What that means is you've got to be ready to take the opportunities that come your way, or go in search of them. As a young manager you can answer the call of companies looking for people they can invest in to build their international reach. "You've got to just take them out there and get them the experience," Kealey says of his team that he sends abroad. "For us we had to build a lot of local teams, and hire people in those local cultures who could help us understand the market and build relationships, but somebody from headquarters also needs to go out there and learn it."

CEOs are looking for the kinds of people who are ready to roll up their sleeves and adjust to the unknown. "You have to be adaptable," Kiran Mazumdar-Shaw told me. "You cannot say 'I come from America, I've got this great pedigree, and therefore I demand you do things certain ways.' No, you have to earn your stripes, not demand it. For instance, I hired my head of R and D who is a guy who came back from the U.S. and was from Genentech. He adapted and changed the way things were done. He was able to get himself accepted." She gave another example of someone who came from the United States, adapted, and integrated himself into the environment. "Now he's also showing people how to do things differently, and he's making that change."

Goodbye, Corporate Headquarters

Most companies still have centralized management and headquarters, but that will change if what Lenovo is doing is any pointer. "We're embracing a strategy we call worldsourcing," Bill Amelio told me. "We think it's the next evolution of globalization. Worldsourcing is an approach to business that defies traditional boundaries, borders, and organizational structures to make maximum use of all the dispersed resources of a company. For example, it's old-fashioned to have a headquarters location with a completely limited perspective. You can see your office, a few cubicles, a single city. Our company is completely global and this system would not work for us. We are bringing together East and West in a new way. Our leaders travel so much. Having a centralized headquarters would not make sense. So we're essentially moving between Beijing, Hong Kong, Singapore, Raleigh, and Paris, the major spots at which we have our meetings. And its working."

For Amelio, it comes down to practicality and diversifying. "The idea of worldsourcing is that you should figure out how to have the majority of resources in the most efficient place possible. You do it in such a way so that you can grow talent wherever it's best available. You want to be flexible and fast moving, so you can't become so heavily positioned in one place that you can't adjust when it's competitively advantageous. If you set the organization up right and doing things in the most logical spot because it's the most efficient and cost-effective, you've got a great opportunity to be able to win."

In Amelio's mind this can be applied not just to human resources but to all departments in the company. "Our ideas come from everywhere and anywhere. We have hubs of excellence located around the world to handle design, key corporate functions, sales, and manufacturing. Ideas flow through the company and into the marketplace as great products and solutions. As an example, we have a centralized marketing hub. We've moved the marketing from all over the world into India. All of our global marketing is developed there, for products that are designed and built worldwide. It's a perfect example of taking globalization to the next conceptual level with worldsourcing."

When I brought up this concept with other executives, most agreed that, indeed, "corporate headquarters" will become a thing of the past. Todd Stitzer of Cadbury Schweppes emphasized the size and scale of his company. "Our company has seventy thousand people, four regional headquarters, and over one hundred manufacturing sites," he said. "You need to be in touch with all of those places, in a balanced and prioritized way. Our own corporate headquarters has a little over one hundred people in it, so networking yourself to the future in that is not worth it." To help ensure that his staffers are prepared for their next steps, he says, "I encourage people in our company to work in a different country at least once. And by virtue of participating in international cross-functional groups, get those experiences."

For Kiran Mazumdar-Shaw, the changing concept of "headquarters" is also relevant for efficient use of time, company resources, and people's health. She especially feels it with board meetings. "I always say to people, 'Why do we need to waste so much time and effort and money on getting everyone to have a board meeting in Bangalore? Why can't we just have a videoconference and a board meeting? But that's not allowed. So my board members who are in the U.S. and U.K. have to fly down to India. And what a chore it is, and a health hazard also, because it does impinge on your health to keep taking all of these trips. Boston to Bangalore is not exactly an easy ride."

United Colors of Business

It is important that you also get a clear grasp of what globalization actually means, the shifting locus of economic growth and the changing patterns of trade and investment. International know-how "is absolutely critical," Sanjiv Ahuja of Orange told me. "Just look at where the global economy is. China is now our third-largest economy. It is a must-have because local countrycentric businesses will always remain small. The only country that can have very large business by itself is the U.S. And now maybe China and India, given the size of their economies. But otherwise, Europe by itself—450 million people—is a third the size of China in terms of the number of people, and in thirty years . . . all of the European economy will probably be the size of the Chinese and Indian economies put together. You can't miss that."

Nandan Nilekani echoed those sentiments. "Over the next fifty years we're going to see some major realignment in the world," he told me. "The fact that poor countries like India and China are growing means that the world economy is going to change, which means that growth is going to happen differently. For any global country, these markets will be very important. For many companies, now global sales are bigger than their U.S. sales. That trend is going to continue and therefore you need somebody who has got the live experience of these markets. In many senses, these countries are the sources for your future employees. So whatever way you look at it, even if your endgame is to become the CEO of General Electric or Hewlett-Packard, then going through this at some point in your career is, in my view, more and more vital."

Indeed, while it seems natural that the CEOs I spoke to who are based outside the United States would stress so acutely the changing world economics, CEOs of U.S.-based companies also agreed with Nilekani. "Unless you're in a very unique industry, it's likely you're going to have to deal with global customers, global supply chains, global suppliers," Bill Swanson of Raytheon told me. "Whatever you're in, you're going to have to deal with global trends. Not to have a strong [international] perspective, I think, is a disqualifier. It is imperative."

"I could be biased by the industry I'm in, which is communications, but your competitors are going to come from all over the world," John Kealey told me. "The fact that we are in satellite communications takes that to an even higher level, because there's no concept of 'local' in satellite distance. But I think that even if your business is more local, still the people you're going to serve are probably going to come from all over the world. Even if they're in the U.S., they will probably need you to support them around the globe."

Ben Verwaayen, who, as we learned earlier, answers all his own e-mails, is a keen blogger. He wrote from Davos—the host city of the World Economic Forum, where the world's elite political and business leaders gather every year—in 2007: "I am interested in how business leaders can seize the fantastic opportunity that we have been given to recruit people from anywhere in the world now that computers link us all together. There is a new meaning to the word *diversity*. We no longer look to just gender mix, or age profile, but to the possibility of embracing ideas, cultures, and experiences from every part of the world. . . . It is great to look around Davos and not just see white men in dark suits. And each year the mix gets richer."

Join the trend, or you won't be getting to that corner office properly equipped, if at all.

Build Your Corporate Culture at Home to Combat Culture Shock Abroad

To Bill Swanson, preparing for increased international business starts at home—*respect* is a term he used frequently to describe the corporate culture he is trying to build and foster. He has instituted a training system where employees learn core values to follow. It consists of a feedback system to help employees see what they're doing right and what they need to work on, and to help them plan their careers. This is essential for a global marketplace. "It resonates across not only our employee base domestically but internationally," he told me. "What happens is that you have to realize that the cultures in the United Kingdom are different from the ones in Australia or in Asia or in the Middle East. But respect is universal. It's global."

And respect is more than just being polite and tolerant. It can be as practical as not making a big fuss about being jet-lagged when you're in someone else's time zone. CTPartners operates in eleven countries outside the United States, and this is how the company's CEO, Brian Sullivan, puts it: "The art of learning how to sleep is a key component to the success of a global CEO. Being available, being part of their day-to-day work lives and caring about those partners and customers as much as your local market is a requirement for success." So don't think of other centers as foreign outposts. "You have to plan your time so that people know when you're going to be in their region and what your expectations are. Being visible on-site is critical to success. Why should people care about what's important to you if you don't care about what's important to them?" This has both practical and intellectual implications: "Appreciate [other cultures'] style, customs, and daily timetable. Everyone is proud of their culture. If [global CEOs] cannot or do not embrace the local culture, they should get the hell out of the country," said Sullivan.

The best place to start, as with most things of this nature, is at home. And training is the best way to do it. Train your executives to be sensitive to cultures outside the country of their residence. Too many global teams have come apart simply as a result of a misdirected insensitive remark. Indeed, once you're in the C-suite, the more you work it into your company's culture to make global training a priority, the better positioned you'll be. That's what Nadia Zaal at Al Barari is doing as well. "I'm already looking at all the people and making sure management attends each other's meetings so they actually start looking [at issues] globally," she said.

Get to Know the New Asia

A list of the world's most important economies used to consist of the United States, Europe, China, and Japan. Now people quickly correct you if you do not add India. But to understand India's importance in detail, it's important to go beyond the "India's the next big thing" level.

Nandan Nilekani explained India's importance. "India is entering a period of what people think is a long secular cycle of growth," he told me. "This has come up for various reasons—because of a freer economy and because of the demographics. India is a young population when the rest of the world is aging, and India is growing when other countries are maturing. Entrepreneurship is being revitalized, technology is becoming available, which India has learned how to use well, and . . . English is the common language, which is also the language of global business. So all these unique things we believe have created the environment for a long secular growth pattern. It creates enormous opportunities."

The numbers are pretty astounding. "If the economy is growing at ten percent a year," Nilekani told me, "what that means is that per capita incomes run from $500 to $1,000, they go from $1,000 to $2,000 and $5,000 over the next three years." This is a direct result of employee supply and demand necessitated by the overall growth of the economy. Evidence of this is that India now has the largest middle-class population in the world. Nilekani continued, "Now, the moment that happens, and as long as they're able to spend this equitably, you have a billion people who go from an income of $1,000 to $5,000. That's an enormous change. It creates opportunities for goods and services because they'll all be consumers. They will buy things, not only products, but they'll buy services, education, health care, telecommunication, and so forth. This fundamental secular growth is therefore creating opportunities for businesses. I think to be a leader in this environment requires leadership that knows how to handle and anticipate growth. The ability to deal with this growth becomes a very critical attribute for the C-suite in these markets. The way you manage in a mature economy is different than the way you manage in a growth economy. In some sense, the technology guys in the West learned to deal with it because in the high-bull manias, they grow like this."

Several executives essentially said to prepare for the wild ride that expansion into India will provide. "There's a lot of excitement for people looking at India because it's such a great growth story," Kiran Mazumdar-Shaw told me. "Obviously people want to be where the excitement is, where the growth opportunities are. I think that's what's attracting people to have an experience of working with an Indian company." Mazumdar-Shaw also pointed out to me that part of the interest (and necessity to expand) in India is in contrast to what's going on in people's home countries. "I think people are excited because in their own regions they're not seeing this kind of growth opportunity. In fact they are very despondent and extremely discouraged and disappointed with the lack of opportunities, and a constant fear of being out of a job. You're getting a pink slip on Monday morning, companies likes Pfizer are cutting jobs, and all the time you're hearing that the most successful companies suddenly are up for sale." In short, Mazumdar-Shaw said, if you are a young manager charting your career, get yourself to India. "India is far more exciting and a far more secure story for them."

Ron Williams of Aetna told me he had recently been in India learning about the country. "We've been principally a domestic business today and we have a small but rapidly growing global activity. One of the things I did recently was to spend a considerable amount of time in India. To go and personally understand what it's like if it's Bangalore, Mumbai, Delhi," he said. "Part of the program was to say, 'Do I have a firsthand contextual feel for what we should be doing in order to operate in the world the way it will be tomorrow, as opposed to the way it was fifteen or twenty years ago?'"

This is true for other parts of Asia as well. Our offices in Singapore, Hong Kong, and Shanghai have all grown tremendously as a result of the competition for talent in the region. It is important to realize that business is conducted differently in the various countries of the region. Although an executive in Singapore may not be offended by you if you just use your right hand to offer him your business card, he will certainly warm up better to you if you offer it to him with both your hands, as is the local custom. These are vibrant economies that continue to grow. You are at a distinct disadvantage if you do not know how to conduct business in them.

Hire a Cultural Translator, So to Speak

One of the first ways to start to go global, of course, is to learn a language. (Sanjiv Ahuja suggested making sure your children learn Mandarin, and he was only half-joking.) But understanding the culture extends far beyond words. It's well known that going into a foreign country, many of the unspoken communication patterns can be baffling.

"You can learn the language, but it's not purely a language issue," said Lee Hsien Yang. "Asians are not always as direct as Americans are," Lee said. "Americans tend to say it like it is, and call a spade a spade. In Asia, sometimes people don't want to tell you they don't agree with you, so they just don't respond. And then you assume they said nothing, and that the idea is okay. People respond in a different way, and if you don't understand what's being said, you get into trouble. Just having the language [skills] doesn't mean you understand what people are saying. You can't read it yourself as a manager coming in from elsewhere. Find somebody you can rely on who can help give you advice."

That is not to say you shouldn't try to soak up as much as you can first. "You have to make an effort to learn enough to be comfortable," Lee advised. "And then after that, you really need to immerse yourself and find a way to make reliable judgments in situations that you're not accustomed to."

Goh Sik Ngee of Yellowpages.com pointed out to me that even though he's based in Singapore, much of Asia remains a mystery even to people who were born and raised there. "A lot of people say that being Chinese there is a natural advantage, and I say yes, to an extent," Goh told me. "But the Chinese in middle China and the Chinese in Singapore are very different. The culture is also very different. We do not assume that just because you look Chinese, you can go there and make friends, and do business in China. It's more than just the ability to speak Mandarin, too. You need to be culturally balanced. You need to read more of the Chinese classical books, for example, history, and things like that. Likewise in India. The culture and history are important factors."

Not Just a Language Barrier

It's well known by now that working internationally, you'll have a host of unforeseen problems, with infrastructure, politics, and the weather, just to name a few potential hazards. Nandan Nilekani gave me some examples of differences he experiences in India that U.S.-based CEOs might be unprepared for—and what you would be wise to prepare yourself for. "We have to deal with what Western companies don't have to," he told me. "Our environment outside is poorer, the infrastructure is poorer, the governance is poor. So the challenge is, how do you maintain and create a high quality inside this not-so-high-quality environment? Everybody has to think differently." In fact, first impressions can be intimidating. The drive from the air-port to your office may be as short as ten miles, but it may take you two hours to commute that distance. An approval process may take months. You need to know how to legally circumvent the system and show results. How do you do that? For one, watch Indian leaders. Nilekani told me that working in India has made him more resource-ful. "Because of the shortage of resources, you learn to be innovative and smarter in the use of your resources," he said. "I've learned that with many Indian leaders. They know how to get a lot done with lit-tle. Sometimes in the best environment where there's a lot of every-thing, it's not like it's a big thing, but here you learn to do things in a much more frugal manner."

Sometimes the challenges are even more daunting than India's infamous infrastructure problems, especially when they are ephem-eral and difficult to understand. When I spoke to Nadia Zaal about executive decision making, I found there was something going on that most other executives didn't have to contend with. Almost every-one else embraced the idea of admitting when you are wrong, but for Zaal it was another matter entirely, even when she felt like the others. "I've noticed that if I've made a decision, and someone tells me after the fact and I can actually correct it and it would probably be in the best interest of the company to do so, I don't, because I just feel like you need to show decisiveness and you need to, like I say, lie in the bed you've made."

How far do you take that? I asked her. Would you bet the company on something like that? "No. No, definitely not. I'm talking about day-to-day matters or things that are not of significant consequence."

Is that a cultural thing unique to the Middle East? I asked. At first she was not entirely sure, but as she explored the feeling further, it became apparent to her that it is. "It very much depends on the audi-ences because I think, especially in this region, there's definitely a perception of what a CEO and decision maker, what a leader, should be. I'm not saying that that's the correct way, but there is that element—you need to command respect from these people."

I told her what almost every other executive had said on this subject—that it is not only good for the company (and the CEO) to admit when you think you've made a mistake, but also important to remedy it. I asked her whether she felt that a CEO making a wrong decision gains more respect from an employee than a CEO reversing her decision to make it correct.

She responded, "I would definitely say it is cultural. I think it's changing a lot, but you know there is a mask sometimes you have to put on because that's what is expected of you."

This is not a circumstance peculiar to the Middle East alone. From Japan, right across Asia, parts of Europe and on to Africa, "losing face" is an issue that distorts communication in all walks of life. People often say it is an Asian thing, but you will find it everywhere. It just has slightly different manifestations in different places. Together with all sorts of other matters related to hierarchy, religion, and history, status plays a big part in the way things are done, from kindergarten to government. And companies are no exception.

"Indian managers deal with multiple backgrounds, religions, castes, and languages," Nandan Nilekani told me. "I think that ability to blend into a diverse environment—diverse and chaotic—is valuable."

Goh Sik Ngee said that for companies that are more spread out and don't have the traditional corporate headquarters that Bill Amelio and others are phasing out, serious misunderstandings can arise. "In one of my previous jobs, the company had offices in twenty-six different cities worldwide, and a lot of those offices are joint ventures with a lot of people, sometimes out of necessity, and sometimes because of the local statutory requirements," Goh said. "You realize that half of the problems we resolved are not about business but in dealing with the residual parties. A lot of the issues arose because of technical understanding. So, [it's] unlike in the past when you are from Singapore [and] you have a very homogenous composition of a team—you all speak the same language and enjoy interacting with people who think like us and behave like us. It's quite easy." The moment you have someone from a different country, everything changes.

Sik Ngee gave an example of working with a Japanese partner or company. "They are very polite, and you may have thought, 'I have agreement,' but [you] do not. In terms of culture, the Japanese are very seniority conscious. Their senior people tend to be older, so you will never find a forty-year-old CEO. Their CEO will have gray hair and be a very elderly person. So if you send in a young guy who could not deal with him, you are in trouble. He does not want to hear a young guy. He wants to deal with a guy who also has gray hair. It's small things like this that if you do not understand you will always have a problem." Goh also said that people tend to hire like people, who speak, behave, even eat the same thing as them, because they feel comfortable with them. "I think CEOs should break away from that."

It works the other way around, too. I asked Seturaman Mahalingam, chief financial officer of Tata Consultancy Services, India's biggest outsourcing company, what were some of the frustrations Indian executives find in the global marketplace. He said they found the working environment was "too structured—meetings and conferences all the time." Related to that is the tendency of companies in Europe and North America to have strict working hours, which means it is often difficult to get ahold of someone outside those hours.

I asked Mahalingam, who was a panelist at a Deloitte conference in Athens, Greece, with me, what advantages Indian executives had over their global counterparts. There were three, he said: India has had a higher emphasis since childhood on education; Indian executives have a hunger to succeed globally; and they give a lot more priority to work and are therefore more passionate. Against this, he said, Indians tend to be indecisive and less able to delegate than their global counterparts. They also need to work on their self-confidence. "Coming from a paternalistic/feudal society, this is an area for attention," he said.

For the young, aspirant executive, there are many areas for attention. You're never going to grasp the subtle nuances of scores of societies around the world—it takes a lifetime getting to really know a second culture after your own, and indeed, most of us are still trying to work out what's going on at home. But what you do need to do is travel enough and spend enough time in other countries and with other cultures—it doesn't particularly matter which—to sensitize yourself to the fact that half of what you say can be misunderstood and half of what you hear is not what you are being told. Once you know this about one society, you'll be alert to it in another. And it is the ability to be alert to these things that matters and will keep you learning and understanding the world, because if you don't know it's happening, you won't do anything about it, and if you do—well, as a good leader you will find out what you need to know to make the right decision.

Executive Summary

Add more stamps to your passport. The more you see of the world, the better off you are. Experience different cultures yourself, and observe the people, customs, and business practices—and come away with a map of the pitfalls. Where you can, school yourself on the complex cultures and incredible diversity among people, languages, and customs even within a country. Learn a new language, and get to know the unspoken cultural barriers as well.

Try to get a job abroad, and when you go, be adaptable. Bosses love people who are at the ready to learn and take on challenges abroad. Be that person, and when you are, don't expect your career to be handed to you. Be ready to adapt and work hard.

Understand other big economies, especially India and China. Learn the details of the Indian and Chinese economies and their place in the world, where they get their resources from, where they are expanding, what they are good at, and what opportunities they offer companies from all over the world.

Get ready for a ride. International expansion is uncharted territory for many people. Stay open (and patient), and expect regional challenges, bureaucracy, infrastructure limitations, and long lines at airports. It will not be easy, but treat it as an exciting adventure that is part of your journey to the top.

Chapter 7

Get a Life—and Keep It

When I asked Ben Verwaayen of BT Group what advice he would give young managers, one of the first things he said was, "You're not what's on your business card. Please don't sacrifice your private life." It was a disarming statement from someone with so much corporate clout. But in fact I found in my conversations with CEOs that no matter how large or successful someone's company was, the issue of the balance between work and personal life provoked considerable concern. In Verwaayen's case, it was fairly straightforward: have a life, which for him includes being a passionate soccer fan (he's an Arsenal supporter) and spending Saturdays with his young grandson and cooking French and Thai meals with his former high-school sweetheart and wife of thirty-one years.

But for many CEOs, such balance can be hard to find. When I asked Brian Sullivan, CTPartners' CEO, whether work-life balance was just a cliché, he replied: "Work-life is real—balance can be sorely missing."

Probably the most unyielding remarks on the subject came from Bill Nuti of NCR. It wasn't by any means the way many, or even most, of the executives I interviewed would have put it, but I suspect a number might have reluctantly agreed with Nuti's comments on the subject: "It's a cliché. Don't let anybody ever kid you. Anybody who ever tells you in this job they have work-life balance, I think they're lying. To me, it's a twenty-four-by-seven job. You've got to be on all the time, whether you like it or not, and it's part of the job. If there's any part of the job I dislike the most, it's the impact it has on my family life and the things I like to do for fun and taking care of myself physically."

Indeed, when I asked Nadia Zaal of Al Barari what she feels she would like to learn as a CEO, she laughed heartily and said, "The one thing I would love to learn right now is how to have balance in my life. I have none."

Todd Stitzer of Cadbury Schweppes thought it was not something you should let go by default because getting it right was an important part of being a good leader. "The notion of balance in terms of spirit, mind, and body is something you have to work very, very hard to try to keep touch with," he said. "I think if you seek to do it all, if you don't save time for your family and yourself, and your physical well-being, you will become a less effective leader."

So how do you do it? JCPenney's Kenneth Hicks said he recently advised a friend who was about to take on a senior management role that there were three things he needed to keep in mind "if you don't want to wind up with a problem." The first, he said, is "you need to set appointments aside with your spouse or family and say, 'We're going to do this. We're going to go to the ball game, or we're going to go out to dinner here, or we're going to do this.' And make appointments, just like you would with business, so that you don't say, 'Yeah, yeah, we'll get to that.' Because it never happens."

The second thing, said Hicks, was to make sure that every day you have some time with your family. He and his wife, Lucille, don't have children, and he concedes that it must be even more difficult for those who do, but says that "one of the things that my wife and I do is we go out to eat every night. And we do it so that we're together and we have time together every night.

"And the third thing is make sure that you take vacations—you have to be able to recharge because the people who say, 'I haven't been on a vacation in five years,' they can't be that brilliant."

Hicks said he also tells people to get a hobby. "I rode horses up until I came here, and so I'm missing that. But I do exercise every day. You have to have something that you can do, whether it's golf, tennis, riding horses, painting, or some other important thing."

That said, what you do about your nonwork life and how you do it is a function of many other things and can change for all sorts of reasons, so don't get anxious if you are not getting the balance quite right. Just be aware of it and try out new strategies. "The individual must make a choice, and the choice is not permanent or irreversible," Goh Sik Ngee of Yellowpages.com told me. "In life our commitments vary according to different phases of life. So when the children are younger, you tend to need to spend more time. When children reach a certain age, maybe it is okay now [that] I am freer, to give one hundred percent of my time." Think about some of your career choices now and how they fit into your lifestyle presently—take those foreign assignments now if you don't have children, or start to think strategically about your spouse's career goals so that your choices can dovetail.

There is much to consider, and it isn't small stuff. If you neglect your family's health now, it may come back to haunt you. More than one CEO I spoke to was frank about the stress that their career imposed on their family. You're embarking on a serious journey, and the more intact the various elements of your life are, the better you will succeed in all aspects, not just the boardroom. Just remember that maintaining your personal life is just as rigorous a task as maintaining your résumé.

Russ Fradin of Hewitt has been married for more than twenty years. The fact that his wife also happens to be a marriage and family therapist might have something to do with the fact that he makes solid choices with their marriage in mind. For example, he takes great pains when organizing his travel schedule. "One of my rules is never to be away for a week," he told me. "It's not good for a marriage, and it's not good for a business. If I go to London or Europe I'll leave on a Sunday and be back on Wednesday."

The frankness with which the executives addressed this issue revealed a genuine struggle and some pain. On the one hand, they wouldn't be in the kinds of jobs they were in if they weren't the first one in, the last one out, and sometimes the only one to stick up their hands. On the other, executives are people, too—and so are their spouses and their children and their aging parents. There is no easy balance, and no one tried to make it sound like there could be. Rick Dreiling, someone who has been in the C-suite for as long as anyone, explained it like this: "I think my wife would say this—and I'm sure you know, I think it's pretty fair—CEOs start off as stock clerks and finance people, and the drive that gets them to become a CEO was there when they were a stock boy or a store manager. That same element is still there." Incidentally, Dreiling and his wife, Ellen, have a son, RJ, and a daughter, Amy. His hobbies are reading and playing golf. He is also an avid auto-racing fan.

"So I can look at you and say how I work," he continued, "and what I throw against it goes back to when my kids were very young. I didn't see every home run my son hit but I saw his first one. And I saw the one that he hit in the championship. I saw my daughter's first basket. Didn't see every basket, but I can honestly say I was there when it counted. And I think that you have to be able to keep your family life and your business life in perspective. I'm fond of telling my people there is nothing more important than your family. Now, I'm a close second, but I ain't first. We work really hard on that. I do mean it. My general counsel has two young sons and it's Friday and I will look at her and say, 'Now do they have a soccer game or something that we should be going to?' And she'll go, 'Well, you know, as a matter of fact, I'm in charge of donuts or whatever they do for the kids' break.' And I'll say, 'Then why don't you get out of here a couple of hours early and make sure the donuts are really fresh.'"

In this chapter I discuss the ways executives try to do it all, from making it to their kids' soccer games, to keeping up with volunteering activities, staying fit, sleeping enough—and running a company. Perhaps a good place to start is with Ben Verwaayen's rather Zen perspective: "You need to have a life which is balanced, but balance doesn't mean the number of hours that you work. Many of those definitions are fatal. Balance is whether you are at peace with yourself."

Do the Math

I asked John Kealey of iDirect, whose office walls display drawings by his children, how he does it. "You can find a lot of ways in your business to measure success," he said, and that is how he approaches the work-life balance question. He broke it down and analyzed it, and devised metrics. "I had to really define for myself, what do I mean by that? Am I going to the kids' field-hockey games and soccer games? I looked at a season and said, 'Hey, how many of these games am I actually making? What percentage of the time am I traveling?' And then, I looked at my schedule and said, 'When am I doing things that clearly could be done by somebody else in the senior management team?' What you find as a CEO is there is never an end to the number of things you'd be doing, so you'd better find some metrics in life—even your personal life—and say, 'Do I think I'm home enough, do I think I'm attending enough of these events?'" Kealey put his kids' soccer, field hockey, and football games on his calendar, so he is sure to know which ones he missed and which ones he got to. "If I'm on the road, I look at my appointments in my BlackBerry, and I know if I've missed one."

Once he figured that out, Kealey said, he had to be really honest with himself. "Am I at the soccer game or on the BlackBerry?" Kealey often asks himself. "My wife, bless her heart, gives me lots of coaching, too. She'll ask me many times, 'Where are you?' and I'll say, 'I'm right here.' She'll say, 'No no no. Mentally, where are you?' And I'll realize I'm at work. So it's good to have a mirror you can look in. You can—without going crazy on your family—find some metrics there."

Being in two places at one time, physically and mentally, isn't an uncommon phenomenon, of course, and Steve Shindler knows it well, too. "As much as it's important to be able to have downtime, and believe me, I try to get my fair share of it with trips with my family [he and his wife, Mary Kay, have three children], while I'm there [work] is always in my head. We were in Montana white-water rafting with my kids and had a great time, but I have to admit that at times, floating down the river, I had thoughts in my head as I'm paddling in the water about remembering to contact this person when I get back."

As Brian Sullivan summed it up, "If you tell some CEOs that they are expected to work forty hours a week and go home, they'll quit. As long as companies have an appreciation for different styles and different work life behavior, let it go. . . . Anyone not aware of what their own personal requirements are probably wouldn't change them regardless."

Remember Your Commitments

Hearing some executives talk about it is a reminder that company and family play similar roles in an executive's life. It's like being called about an emergency by a close family member when you are in the middle of something important. It is hard to ignore them and ask them to call you later. "You always hear the phrase 'We're a twenty-four/seven organization,'" said Shindler, "and I think in this job you can wholly commit to that emotionally, spiritually, physically—not that you're actually working that number of hours on a consistent basis, but the mind-set is there. Being available to that extent is so that the organization, stakeholder base—whether they are shareholders, creditors, vendors, or employees—know that you're always thinking about how to make the business better, and that you can be called upon to provide that input. You're going to be there when those tough decisions need to be made. You can't ever have a meltdown. You can't say you're tired and I want some real time away where you fully disconnect from the business." In other words, as a CEO, you have two families in effect. The decisions you make about spending time with one will have significant effects on the other.

"Start with the fact that you are taking on an obligation that goes beyond yourself and your own family," Ron Williams told me (he has been married for more than twenty years and has one son). "It's an obligation to, in our case, thirty thousand employees who are here today. It's an obligation to our customers and our shareholders. And to society at large. You have to understand and be comfortable taking on that obligation. Once you do that, you understand that it may well take precedence over other obligations."

To put it in perspective, Williams compared his role to that of his employees. "They don't go to fancy dinners, they don't come to meetings, they don't get to vote on whether we should pursue this strategy or that strategy, or how we solve problems. They're counting on the senior executives of the company to be diligent, to put our time in and to ask and figure out what we should be doing in order to help the business grow, make the business be profitable, and give them a stable growing place that they could be employed. To me, it starts with that as a fundamental understanding. That would mean you may miss a family event here or there or a party, or there may be things you have to work around."

Nadia Zaal had the most uncompromising view of what she expected of her team. Perhaps it is her youth, perhaps it is the fact that she expected of them the same commitment that she has to the company. Whatever the reason, she was characteristically open about it: "I expect people's job to come first . . . over anything else: family, friends, social life, especially because of the stage where the company is now, because we're a young company, there's so much to do, I just expect that, and I'm very clear about it. I say to people, 'Listen, over the next two or three years, you know, you have no life. You either accept it or you don't.' "

Get Your Family on Board

The more supportive your spouse is, the better, because the fact is, he or she is going to share some of the burden. "If you're married, it has to be a joint effort, because a lot of the times the extra work you're putting in to try to build something is extra work that your spouse is trying to do to keep the family together," Bob Reynolds of Fidelity told me. It helps if your spouse understands your industry, although not everyone is as lucky as Reynolds, whose wife worked in the 401(k) business at T. Rowe Price. "She knew what it was all about, and she knew the game and was totally on board," Reynolds told me.

"Every once in a while she would say, 'Do you have to be out five nights a week?' or 'Well, why do you have to have dinner with [a colleague]? You see him every day.' Those are the times you really get to know people or get after issues. I do think it's an understanding from a partner standpoint about what it takes to get to the level that you want to go."

"It has to work [with] the family," Ron Williams of Aetna said. "You can't want to go one way and have other family members that want to go another way. Your family has to sign up for what you are attempting to do and recognize that you can't do everything, that you can do important things and that sometimes when you plan something, something else may come up. But it shouldn't preclude you from doing everything. It's an impingement factor, and when that obligation calls you have to be responsive to it."

Indeed, Sanjiv Ahuja of Orange told me "there wasn't a chance in hell" he could have gotten to where he did without his wife's help. "I didn't realize how big a sacrifice a wife would have to make as I go through the journey," he said. "I don't know if I would put up with it. In many ways your spouse makes bigger sacrifices. You are engaged in activity and your spouse is carrying the entire load that you used to be carrying. So they pay a big price, and they're not valued at all in the perception of what they do." While executives get public acclaim for a job well done, the spouse relies entirely on you to get kudos for important work being done at home without your help.

Some executives told me that if the roles were reversed, they don't know if they could have done it.

Questions about whether you make it to your child's hockey game are not simply about scheduling. Some of them are about your life and theirs, about key moments in their development. "You don't get to spend time with your children, and you miss out on a very big phase of your life which is outside work," Ahuja told me. "The first dance recital, first athletic award. You miss all of those. And by the time you slow down you're in your mid-sixties, kids are grown up, and you're looking at grandkids."

Of course, the trade-off is that you're contributing to the world at large through your work, even if you sacrifice some at home. "You can make a significant difference when you're in a big leadership position. But don't be surprised with those trade-offs," Ahuja warned. "The more you think through it you make a conscious trade-off, and when you get your next big promotion or big assignment in a different geographical location, make sure you spend enough time at home, with your kids, and enough time alone thinking through whether this is the right thing."

Steve Shindler of NII Holdings says you must be honest and prepare your family for those times. "The hardest part is when we have streaks of intense international travel and it usually comes around the same time we have investor conferences and vendor meetings," he said. For him, September and October, and March and April are his busiest times. "We don't have to travel the rest of the year, but those are the ones that are most intense to the point where I'm on the road virtually every business day and a decent number of weekends as well. It's equally as hard on the spouse because they are dealing with the brunt of all the typical family and emotional issues. You call and try to portray how your difficult day of meetings is going, and they don't want to hear about that. They want to vent on the stuff that they're trying to take care of, which seems trivial at the time when you're trying to make million-dollar decisions." Just understand that their job is as important, if not more important, as yours.

Reorganize Your Schedule

Russ Fradin uses what he calls "time shifting" when he tries to fit everything in. He puts in all the hours he needs to, just not necessarily within the confines of the standard business day. E-mail helps him to fit in extra work at odd hours so he can make time for other priorities. "I have no problem leaving the office at four-thirty, coaching my kids' Little League game, having dinner with the family, and then I'd be back on the computer at nine-thirty and work for another three hours," he told me. "But I get less sleep. I work out at five in the morning."

And if you do more than just work out to stay in shape, but have a time-consuming sporting interest, you have to think strategically. "If your family and business are your top priority and you love to play soccer on weekday or weekend mornings with a group of friends, you probably have to give up the soccer," Todd Stitzer told me. "Or you have to do it at a time when it isn't intruding on your family or business life. I found myself looking for a method of physical fitness that takes an hour as opposed to three or four or five hours. You need to satisfy yourself that you're seeking balance and recreation and cultural stimulation, but in a way that doesn't sacrifice your family or work, which means you sort of sacrifice your own personal interests for a period."

Likewise, Bill Amelio keeps his outside pursuits to a minimum. "I manage to see my kids and spend as much quality time as I can," he told me. "I don't golf. The only thing I do is work out, and it's a lifesaver for me. I've learned that in any job—and especially a stressful one—you have to take care of your physical and mental well-being. Exercise helps me in practical ways like making adjustments to time zones. It also helps me stay emotionally balanced and intellectually focused. There's plenty of research to support the need to exercise and the right chemical balance in helping you perform, manage stress, and enjoy life."

Steve Shindler does some reorganization mentally, not necessarily hourly. Like Fradin, he tries to get home for dinner, but accepts that he's essentially always working all the time, remembering little things to take care of and working through problems in his head wherever he is. "If I'm playing a game with one of my kids and need to portray to them that I'm fully engaged and to whatever level I need to be, I am," he told me. "I'm giving them my time, but at the same time processing other things that I need to get done. And I've gotten them used to the fact that I'll come home in the evening and spend time with them at dinner and ask about their day and be around generally. If I have reading to do in the evening, I'll make a point of not marching myself off into a separate room. I'll sit with them if they're doing their homework or whatever else they need to do. I'm there, with them, and they know that I'm around, but I'm doing the things that need to get done."

Jim Donald has what at first sight seems a very different approach, though as he talked more about it, I thought other executives would recognize his approach in their own. Characteristically, however, Donald enters the debate like a whirlwind, turning the assumptions and the language inside out. "It's a cliché. . . . Work, life, balance. If you try to balance something, nothing goes up or nothing goes down, right? It just balances. Status quo. Personal life, your professional life, it just sits in the middle. Nothing happens. You can't use work-life balance for anything. What I do . . . is called 'work-life blend.' I heard this term from a consultant. You blend in all the stuff that you need to do personally and professionally and make it work."

He recalled how he was once saying this in a speech "to four hundred marketing executives, and they said, 'Give us an example.' I said, 'I'd love to give you an example.' At the time my son was in the third grade, my younger son, playing baseball. If you watch third graders play baseball it's three hours of pretty boring stuff, right? So I'm in a chair on the third base, right behind third base, with my [laptop] and my notes for the week. And in the time that that game goes on I will answer all of my e-mails, and I'll have it done. Now, when Alex [his son] is up, or when he's in the field, I'm watching. He doesn't know any difference. I used to love those games. My wife would say, 'You gonna take Alex to the game?' 'I'd love to, I can't wait.' And so I'd sit down and I'd bust through all my stuff, and I'd be done for the weekend. That's blending. You're there for your son, you're watching him play, you're cheering him on, but you're also working stuff through."

Donald illustrated his point with another story. "So I was interviewing this guy, and he asked me the same question. And I said, 'Well, let me give you an example,' because on my desk was a note to call a new store manager and congratulate him. I said, 'Let me tell you about work-life blend. You're sitting here. I'm interviewing you, right?' 'Yeah.' 'You ask me this question, I'll show you, live in action.' I put it on speakerphone, call the store manager and congratulate him. He couldn't believe that I'd remembered and that I'd called him. I said, 'See you later, good luck,' and signed off. Then I said to the guy, 'Now, what was the next question?' That's work-life blend."

When Donald first started talking about the work-life thing, it sounded like he was arguing for the side of always putting work first. But here was a whole different way of looking at it. Not that Donald is the first executive to try to get some work in under cover of family-and-friends time. It's just that he is the first person I have come across who was advocating it as a solution rather than admitting to it with regret. "It *is* a solution," he said. "It's how I live my life today. I'm going back and forth to the East Coast, I'm going to the Midwest,

I'm answering all these calls, and I still get up with my son, help him get ready for school. I coach his basketball team still."

"You have time to coach his basketball team?" I asked with astonishment.

"My fifth year," he replied proudly. "It's work-life blend. . . . I have an assistant coach [with whom I] kind of go back and forth if I'm traveling. But for five straight years I've coached him since the second grade to the sixth grade now."

Get By with a Little Help

When figuring out your work-life balance, delegating can help a lot (see chapter 8). "Expect to work long hours, but learn to delegate," John Kealey advised. "One of the things I see in a lot of up-and-coming CEOs is they sometimes feel like they have to do everything, but if you do, the personal sacrifices become untenable. You've got to trust your team to do some things, and you've even got to let them make mistakes."

Bill Amelio looks at his role as that of someone who sets the rhythm and pace of everyday work life, and when we met he was in the middle of what he called putting an "execution culture" in place, helping his employees take ownership of their work and take on more responsibility. Still, he said, "Its about ensuring that as CEO, I don't have to manage every element of every organization. Sooner or later I have to say, 'You're in charge. I'm just going to look over here periodically, because I expect you to do it now. We've talked about it, you know how to do it, and I should be able to break away and be able to get more sanity.'" I asked Amelio exactly how a young manager would do this, and he said, "You have to bring in great talent and organize it effectively. When you have talented people in the right jobs gaining the right experiences and striving to grow, you can accomplish great things." This will free up more of your time.

Keep Up the Extracurriculars

One of the most frequent pieces of advice to young managers that I received from executives I spoke to was to find and maintain outside activities—or you'll go mad. "I would say they should make sure they have plenty of time to do the things they need to do to keep their sanity or they won't do a good job," Carl Bass told me. "Whether that's reading books or spending time with their children or doing physical activity, people need to do that stuff. You need to be a well-rounded person, in my mind, to do the impossible job."

Volunteering is one such activity. Not only is it fun and helps you contribute to a cause you care about, but a side effect is it will place you in a more positive light. "I treasure people who are involved in community service and charities," Goh Sik Ngee told me. It also gives you a chance to step out of your role and assume another. "As a senior manager or CEO, in our job we tend to [make] demands, but in community work you tend to give, not demand," Goh explained. "You contribute. The rest of the people involved are also volunteers. You do not demand that they contribute. You encourage them, and motivate them. I feel that it makes a person, as a human being, more complete." Those who report directly to you may also view you differently. "I think as a CEO, besides leading the ship you are also a role model for your people," Goh said. "For example, if I deal with bosses [who] have years of volunteerism in charity work, I would view them differently. I would respect them much more, as a more complete person. A contribution to society is something I would expect of senior people."

Just Say No

Several executives stressed that the really successful leaders know how to say no. Plain-speaking Ben Verwaayen told me that when people say they work 24/7, it's "nonsense." "It's just macho advertising," he said. "I can make it twenty-four/seven if I say yes to every invitation that comes to my desk, but I say no to ninety-nine percent. I don't golf, we don't do receptions." Still, he makes time for climate-change work as the chair of the Confederacy of British Industry's Climate Change Task Force, spends time with his grandson, and makes sure he doesn't miss football games. "I have a grandson who's four years old, and if he comes [to visit at home], that's more important than the next meeting," he said. "Now, if a customer wants to see me, I'm there. If there's something important here internally, I'm always there. It's a matter of course." But Verwaayen stays away from the peripheral parts. "Some people love all that stuff, shaking hands, having small talk, but in my judgment, in ninety-nine percent of those cases it's just people occupying the time of other people."

Carl Bass of Autodesk conceded that being a CEO is an enormous time strain. "On the other hand, there's no doubt that you make a huge amount of sacrifice on your time, and that there are times where you have no option but to let in the work world. Emergencies happen, people will call you on Saturday in the middle of the night and you have to do something. [For example], there's an earthquake in Japan and you have to figure out what you're going to do with employees." But he was even more blunt than Verwaayen about the exaggeration that goes on regarding how much time people put in: "Most people who tell you it's a twenty-four/seven job, or that they work eighty, ninety, or one hundred hours a week, [are] full of crap," he said. "Just do the math on it. If you're doing six days it's sixteen-and-a-half-hour days. How long can you really maintain that? If you do it over seven days, it's fourteen hours a day, and I'm not talking about driving in the car. I'm talking about when people say they have worked hundred-hour workweeks, it's hard to do. I also think if you went and looked at anybody's productivity over those long periods, [you would find it goes] down enormously."

If you do find yourself working that much, Bass recommends some self-reflection. "At a certain point you're just doing it for the sacrifice or avoiding other stuff rather than being effective in how you work," he said. One anecdote he told me about a colleague was particularly telling. "There's a guy who was the hardest-working person I've ever met, and he spent more hours here than ever before," he began. "More hours at the office than anyone I knew. Nonstop, on the phone around the world. He would fill up literally sixteen hours a day doing work stuff." At one point he and Bass were both vice presidents, each in charge of different businesses. One Saturday he called Bass to notify him that the parking garage by his building was empty. "Good," Bass replied. The man was baffled that Bass would think it was a positive thing that no one was working on the weekend. Bass told him, "Your motto is 'Why do in five days what I can do in seven?'" This workaholic attitude doesn't resonate with Bass. "My feeling is if people can do their work in a way that's high quality, leads to a sustainable lifestyle, that is far more to be encouraged than trying to figure out how do we have people punch clocks and spend as much time as possible at the office."

Lee Hsien Yang, who is married with three sons, had much the same view as Bass and Verwaayen. "I think most people who eventually get into senior positions realize that some amount of a hard grind is necessary, but you need to find a way to have that balance. You can work thirty-six hours a day if you wanted to, but I think people who do will find that they can't sustain that for very long, which is not to say that from time to time you may not find it necessary to work fairly intensively. But I think that people who really have staying power draw a line and say, 'This is the balance I'm comfortable with. And I'll set aside certain time for certain activities,' whether it's their own personal well-being or the well-being of the family. If you're not prepared to put that aside, then I think you become dysfunctional quite quickly."

A Lopsided Life Could Mean a Lopsided Company

The consequences of working very long hours may be much more than just bags under your eyes. "There are people who for various reasons don't have a life outside of their careers, and sometimes it's not good for the company. Their employees don't like it, either," Lee warned.

Carl Bass said his colleague who worked weekends forced everyone down the ladder to keep up his breakneck pace. "Staff meetings had to be on Saturday morning," Bass told me. "On the day after Christmas and New Year's he would send out an e-mail with stuff to do within an hour of getting up at six in the morning. He would already be on e-mail. In some ways it was just a form of harassment. There was nothing that was useful about it," Bass said, and then added, "His business never did better than mine."

Walt Bettinger was as plain-speaking on this subject as he was on everything else: "If someone has to lose their marriage to be successful, then I don't want to be a leader in that organization. And I don't want to create a business environment that requires those sort of trade-offs. I want an organization [in which] a person could attain any form of significant leadership and be a great husband, or wife or father or mother or partner. Those things shouldn't have to be traded off. And so when I talk with younger up and coming leaders, I talk very explicitly about this."

Drawing as he so often did from life in the armed forces, Kenneth Hicks told of a general who would "require everybody to be gone by six-thirty on Friday night. He said, 'I don't care if you have to come back in at three in the morning on Saturday. Every [Friday] night, if you're married, I want you to be home with the family. If you're single, I want you to be out on a date. And if you can't get a date, I want you at the club having a drink with your friends. But everybody has to have some time that they've set aside so that people know that they can count on this is when we're going to have some personal time.' "

"There are many careers and jobs that inherently can't be balanced," Steve Reinemund told me. "It's part of human nature. And I don't think it's the job that requires it as much as we as leaders and individuals, and humans don't discipline ourselves enough to have balanced lives. It takes constant effort, and it's never perfect." He also noted that he wouldn't necessarily want to be one of his workaholic peers. "I've seen enough people who've 'succeeded' in business whose lives I wouldn't want to emulate. If you think about it, it's not that hard to have a singular focus and be successful. The difficulty is having multiple focuses and achieving that balance."

For Reinemund, only by having a varied life can one be a stronger leader. "A lot of the unbalanced leaders who get to the top have real problems because most people don't want to do that," he said. "They don't respect it and they're not understood by leaders who are singularly focused." The old-school executive does not want to hear excuses about work not being done because of family issues. That trend, he noticed, is changing. "I think increasingly, young people are properly asking that question early, more so than when I was coming out of school. People are saying, 'I want a balanced life and I want to start working at that early on, even if it means I don't get there,' wherever 'there' is. I think that's quite positive."

At the heart of the battle for balance is, of course, time. Terrance Marks of Coca-Cola explained just how important it is to remember that: "I have a strong belief that there's one resource that everybody in my position, or any position, whether you're up here or driving a taxicab, that everybody has in equal amounts. And they can't make any more of it, but they don't have any less of it. And that's time. So treat it like your most precious resource, because you can't get any more, no matter what you do. . . . If you use that resource more effectively than the next person, then you win."

But, he stressed, choosing what you do with your time is just as important: "So you want to be a good . . . family person. You want to be a successful executive. You want to be a scratch golfer. You can't. . . . Pick two. A lot of people have three things that they want to do really, really well. So choose wisely. Just choose with your eyes wide open. There's no right or wrong. We all have our own value systems, but it's up to every individual to choose wisely and then live with the consequences of those choices. But if you want to be really good, my belief is that you should be really good in two things, but you can't be really good—really, really good—in three things. One's going to give. Don't be surprised."

Executive Summary

Get your family on board. Just as it's important to build a strong team at the office, make your family part of your team, too. You're signing up for a huge job with responsibility not only to do the job, but to provide stability and success for every person affected by your business. You *will* have to make huge sacrifices, but you can't do it alone.

Be creative with your time and your schedule. If it means leaving the office early to make it to your child's soccer game, and getting on the home computer to resume work after the kids fall asleep, do it. When you spend quality time with the family, find ways to multitask and solve work problems at the same time.

Delegate. No CEO ever did the job alone. Learn how to delegate, and trust that your staff can take care of tasks that don't require your presence. That way, you can get much-deserved downtime without worry that something will blow up in your absence.

Get out of the office. Volunteer, join nonprofit groups, exercise. Make sure you have outside activities that get you out of your head, and help build skills that will make you a better leader—and may even put you in a better light among your bosses and peers.

Stop working so hard. A relentless work schedule is a vicious cycle. It'll wear you out, your productivity will diminish, and your workaholic tendencies are likely to be unappealing to your closest team members—and make you a less-effective leader. Taking a break will help you be better at your job.

Chapter 8

What's in a Leader?

I asked Rick Dreiling of Duane Reade how you know when you're in a dead-end job. His answer was surprising, and emphatic: "I haven't ever had a job I didn't like, never." He looked at me earnestly and continued, "You know, I always wanted to be the guy that had the best productivity when I was a night stocker. When I was a store manager, I always wanted the biggest sales increase or whatever the focus was on. I always wanted to be the best district manager. So the answer is, I think that a good CEO, or CEOs in general, have the ability to take the hand that they're dealt and turn it into a winning hand. And that's the play."

So it helps if all your life you have wanted to be the best at everything you do. But being the best when you are in charge of a top team of executives and hundreds, perhaps thousands, of employees is different from being the best night stocker, and Dreiling would readily admit this. When he addressed the question "What makes a great CEO?" he pointed to a number of the characteristics that he had amply embodied throughout our interview. He began with one of the great communication skills he commanded himself and that others had stressed in my interviews with them: "I think great CEOs have the ability to take complex issues and boil them down to simplicity. . . . When you hear great CEOs talk, they talk to you almost like they are reading out of the *Reader's Digest.* There are no big words; it's just very clear. It's very concise."

Dreiling went on to list what he sees as the most vital leadership attributes of a successful executive: in addition to clarity, both in the way they communicate and in the way they frame their goals, Dreiling also emphasized the importance of paying attention to the needs of the people working for them. "They have the ability to articulate how people are doing on the journey. They have the time to provide feedback . . . they have the ability to make you feel like you are the most important person on the earth when they are talking to you." There are also those things you would expect—"the drive, the work ethic . . . obviously, most CEOs are pretty smart people." But a big part of being a great CEO is admitting when you don't know something. Dreiling told me, "Even when I deal with my board, I'm not afraid to say, 'I don't know, let me get back to you,' rather than try to BS [my] way through something."

Arthur Collins of Medtronic chose to get around to the question of what makes a great CEO by telling a story from his childhood. He said he vividly remembers the day he and a friend were playing baseball in the street. "One of us hit the ball into the window of a neighbor," he recalled. "Our block wasn't the friendliest neighborhood in the world, so we just scattered. When I came home I must have looked kind of sheepish, because my father could tell something was wrong. 'Well, what happened?' he said. When I told him, he said, 'You go right up to that front door, you ring the doorbell, tell the neighbor, and take your consequences.' I was scared to death."

To this day Collins remembers the moment as if it happened yesterday and he brings that childhood lesson to his job of CEO of an $11 billion medical technology company for which he must be accountable. After all, his shareholders—not to mention millions of customers—depend on it.

Collins spoke for executives the world over. Regardless of industry or position or geography, everyone stressed a basic value system. Traits that are often ingrained in us by our parents are crucial to handling the vast responsibilities of a CEO.

But rite-of-passage experiences occur throughout life. Jim Donald, former CEO of Starbucks, related his big moment in his inimitable storytelling style. It was when he worked for Sam Walton of Wal-Mart. "One of the things that Sam taught me, the biggest, and to me it's the most important step, is 'never be bigger than the front line.' And it rings true today, with all that's going on, that the individuals, particularly at retail who are behind the cash register, are as important as the executives in the executive suites." Walton told Donald this one day by asking him to come see him at a warehouse meeting to talk to the first shift and the second shift. "And at the first shift he was making his point in a warehouse where all the trucks are parked, and as he goes to make a point he reaches into his pocket for some note cards. And when he pulls his note cards out, out come pencils and papers and all this kind of stuff. And he had his fanny pack of cancer medication on, he bends down and very in a weak sort of way puts it all back and he finishes up, and he comes and sits down. And I said, 'Are you okay, Mr. Sam?' And he goes, 'Yeah.' I said, 'Do you want me to do the afternoon one?' And he said, 'No, I'll do it.' And so in the afternoon presentation at the same time doing the same thing everything comes out of his pockets again. He puts it all back; he comes over to me, and he says, 'Do you understand?' And I said, 'I'm not sure.' He said, 'Never be bigger than the front line. I wanted to portray myself as fumbling and bumbling a guy as everybody in this room is.' At the time he was the richest guy in the world. And he said, 'If you want to be successful, never be bigger than the front line.'"

Having such "values-based" guidelines for leadership should not be thought of as understating the importance of the more practical business skills necessary to bring in revenue or build up a global infrastructure or manage a large workforce, but, as Sanjiv Ahuja, former CEO of the mobile-telephone group Orange, told me, "it's much harder to find good leadership than industry skills." Good leaders, he continued, can learn the necessary technical skills.

This came out in many of the interviews when I asked about what someone looks for in a successor (see also chapter 3). Russ Fradin, CEO of Hewitt Associates, used a rather morbid measuring stick: "The question I always ask is, 'If I were leaving all my money and I wanted it to go to my kids, would I trust this person to be the executor of my will?' To me, that's sort of baseline."

And then, of course, a CEO needs to push him or herself intellectually, along with striving for a secure moral sensibility. Steve Reinemund, former CEO of PepsiCo, put it in an almost poetic way, drawing on what he called a "model" of leadership that he had been working on for some time: "I think about it as head, heart, and hands," he told me. "A leader needs to have a strong, sound head; [a] caring and passionate [heart]; and a skilled set of hands."

Without exception, all the executives I interviewed described the same handful of prerequisites for stellar leadership. In a sense the qualities sound basic, but you can never assume one in a leadership position has what it takes underneath it all, and basic virtues and intellect take cultivating. Here I examine the characteristics that make an exceptional leader, as described by the people I spoke to—those who live and breathe it.

Integrity for Hire

Integrity topped the list of the key ingredients of every leader. In today's age of ethical misdoings, it is vital. "You need to have a lot of integrity, and always need to think of the interest of the community" is how François Barrault, CEO of BT Global Services, explained his philosophy.

A CEO must not only exude integrity but try to make it part of his or her personal "brand." "An individual must make sure he's known as someone with high values, integrity, and doing the right thing for the right reason," Ron Williams of Aetna said. But sometimes doing the right thing isn't what everyone else wants—having integrity doesn't always win popularity contests. "You have to be managerially tough in the sense of really confronting difficult decisions," Williams continued. "That ability is important. Not having it doesn't give you the kind of value that's expected at the senior level."

Sanjiv Ahuja of Orange also saw the connection between a person's fundamental values and his or her brand. "Always stand up for what you believe in," Ahuja said. "I'm not saying you should demonstrate inflexibility, but there are some core values, core principles that we as all human beings stand for. What is our brand, individual brand, about? And what establishes that very early in one's life? Be true to that. Everything else will follow."

To Steve Shindler of NII Holdings, integrity comes with the territory and actions arise out of sound thinking in an almost organic way. "[We] want to make the company more successful over time, and that breeds the 'do the right thing' mentality, and keeping the integrity and credibility in check and intact," he said. "Don't try to get around stuff, because that comes back to bite you at the end." Shindler compares his company to a piece of property that you care for. "It's like you own a home, and you want to invest the time and the money in the things that make that home nice. It's something you have to have pride in and not let fall apart."

CMGI's Joseph Lawler felt it was simple: "You know, I think it's not hard, it's not complicated. Number one is, when you make a commitment, live up to it. Whether those are financial commitments, whether those are timelines that you commit to, whether it's 'I'll get something done, here's my sales plan.' Whatever it is, deliver that. But set expectations in a way that you make sure you can deliver it. Don't fall short of your expectations, because that says a lot about you.

"And number two is, make decisions that are just right for the long run. Do things that are good for the long run. People who can't distinguish between what's right and what's wrong never get to the corner suite. So that's usually not a conversation that you have to have. But everybody is tested at some point in their career around right from wrong, black and white from gray. How people sort of work their way through that is a defining moment in their career. Everybody crosses it at some point. Make the decision about what's right."

Arthur Collins also had two values he thought were "almost the ticket to get in the door." He put his thoughts in a memo on Medtronic's CEO selection criteria in 2006. "The two most important leadership criteria in my estimation for a successful CEO are judgment and integrity. And without that I don't think you get to the other ones."

When Collins was asked whether the memo would have been any different if he had written it when he took the job, five years earlier in 2001, he answered, "Probably. I can't tell you exactly how it would have been different. If I'm not a better CEO or probably know more about being a CEO, and being a CEO at Medtronic, today than I did when I took the job, then shame on me. I haven't grown, I haven't learned anything. So I think that, yeah, I don't think I would have been able to write what I had written to the board perhaps in the same way or with as much knowledge or conviction as I wrote it when I wrote it."

Company First

Selflessness is another universal idea that repeatedly came up. Once you've reached the top, it's hard not to let it get to your head—after all, you've worked your tail off, so you deserve to be proud of yourself— but many a company's downfall has been the result of egos getting out of hand. Always remember that "Number 1" is not you; it's the company.

Ron Williams said it well: "My own philosophy is that I'm here to represent the institution, not myself," he told me. "It's my job to make certain that Aetna, as an institution, is well understood, is appreciated for what we bring both to our customers and to other key constituents that we serve." He also addressed a paradox, that of having a strong sense of self as a figurehead of a company, but always remembering what it is he's representing. "Now in our society and the way we structure things, I happen to be the face and voice of the institution and so you have to be prepared to step up and do that, which I'm more than glad to do," he told me. "But it really is about Aetna. It's not about me." Many of the CEOs I've met over the years display this kind of devotion to their companies, and it comes through in the way they run it, and, ultimately, in their personal and professional success.

As a CEO, you're only as strong as your weakest link, and what helps define this key trait of selflessness that many of the CEOs described to me is the willingness to make the same sacrifices yourself that you expect of your team. Fidelity's Bob Reynolds said this: "Never ask anyone working for you to do something you wouldn't do yourself." He said it was a philosophy he put into place in the year 2000, as he anticipated the computer glitches that might happen when the clock struck midnight at the turn of the millennium. "A great example of that was Y2K, where we were asking a lot of the organization [not to take] vacation from November 1 on. Everyone's got to be here on New Year's Eve. In the past most people take off in that period, but the expectation was as a manager, you're going to do exactly what you're asking your people to do. And it's like going after new business—jumping on an airplane all the time. I would never ask someone to do something I wouldn't do. So, if someone said [to me], 'Will you go to California with us on Friday?' I would say, 'Absolutely. Let's go.'" This attitude is key to building a strong team, an essential part of the job that was described in detail in chapter 3.

Some CEOs show a selflessness even in their personal style. I was struck by the simple décor in Ben Verwaayen's office when I visited him. Instead of ostentatious furniture and accessories that announce he's the top dog, his office was decorated simply with three BT Group advertisements and was otherwise functional and reflected his down-to-earth attitude. When our meeting was over, he rode the elevator down with me, and the employees who saw him en route didn't seem fazed to see their CEO escorting me to the lobby. Of course, that is the style that works best for him. I'm not telling you how to decorate your office. Be yourself, but ultimately, keep in mind your company's best interests and how your habits reflect them.

Whatever business your company is in, always think of yourself as serving your company. That's how Walt Bettinger of Charles Schwab described his philosophy. A good measure of what you strive for as a leader is what you value in job candidates. "I first look for people who recognize that aspiring to be a leader is aspiring to serve. I look for folks who aspire to lead as a means of serving other people." If your goal is the rewards of celebrity-fame or money, a leadership role isn't really for you. "Don't chase the reward," Bettinger cautioned, "Or you will be forever disappointed. If you're chasing the opportunity, serve other people to be the type of leader, to be the type of manager, to be the type of human being that others might benefit from. That's what to chase. And the other things may happen or they may not, but the rewards shouldn't be what you chase. That shouldn't be the definition of success."

Be Smart

Intellect counts. "I like people who are smart," John Swainson of CA, Inc. told me when I asked him what he looks for in prospects. "I like people who are open, honest. I like people who have a passion for what they're doing. I don't think anything really replaces, though, being smart. This is a tough industry with a lot of very clever competitors in it. So nothing replaces intellect."

When I spoke to Terry Marks of Coca-Cola he was in the middle of considering moving someone to a new position, and much of what directed his decision was what he called the person's "intellectual horsepower." Indeed, as I spoke to more and more executives it seemed these qualities are part and parcel of the whole person. One trait feeds another, and so on. The person Marks was referring to also had "the right value system and a very strong work ethic." The corporate world will always have its detractors, even its outright criminals, but there is no demand these days for an "evil genius."

When I met with Russ Fradin, he was also in the middle of a candidate search (see chapter 3). He gave an example of the kind of person he would hire over, for example, a Harvard graduate. "When you do recruiting you learn all of these things," he said. "You could get somebody who maybe was a salesperson of copiers, something none of us would ever want to do, who happened to set the sales record for two years in a row." While the candidate might not have an Ivy League MBA, he showed an intelligence Fradin looks for in a top manager. "That kind of person has street smarts and is willing to get the door slammed in their face ten times to get the one yes."

It made me recall Reinemund's "head, heart, and hands" leadership model, which, on the head side, calls for "intellectual horsepower" and experience—not just personal experience, but the ability to learn from the experience of other people.

Be Honest with Yourself

The executives I spoke to did not confuse intelligence or intellect with *knowing*. I once saw a bumper sticker that said, QUICK, EMPLOY A YOUNG PERSON WHILE THEY STILL KNOW EVERYTHING. Executives with experience insist that knowing when you don't know is just as important as having a good brain. In fact, it is the sign of a good brain, since you learn so much more when you say you don't know than when you pretend you do.

Walt Bettinger said he's based his career on honesty with himself, and has noticed the same quality among many of his peers. "I've not yet met the successful businessperson who says they're smarter or better at making decisions than other folks," he told me. "Rather, it requires intellectual honesty." That is, the ability to synthesize information in an analytical way. It also requires an honesty toward other people. "My job as a leader is to ensure that my leadership team consists of people with life experiences, and then it's to foster a world of openness, transparency, honesty, and vulnerability among the team such that we are willing to share with each other what we see and not hoard the part that we can see out of our peripheral vision." Not many students of management would name "vulnerability" in even a long list of qualities desirable in an executive. But in this context you can see its value: in this world it helps you get to where you want to be much more than boldness and brashness.

Before you get too keen on weaknesses, remember the context of all of this. John Swainson agreed that while intellectual curiosity is important, understanding your strengths and weaknesses is, too. Sometimes it's even a matter of realizing you might not be cut out for a certain career path. "I think all of us have constraints and all of us do things better and do things worse," he told me. "Some of us are not very good golfers and I think what you have to be is honest with yourself about what you are and what that qualifies you to do." Even when you get to the top, the best C-suiters know what their strengths are and to what roles and industries they are best suited. This is not about "winging it" with a smile.

Staying true to yourself also means acknowledging that you have your own way of doing things and that at a certain point you do not have to keep looking around for a role model or a mentor. I found most executives whom I asked, "Have you been inspired by people?" tended to shake their heads gently. "Not really," said François Barrault in a typical response. I asked him why he thought so many executives answered this way. "Because I do not need somebody to tell me what to do. One of the reasons is, I do not want to look like somebody else. There is nobody [about whom] I say, 'I want to be this guy.' I say I want to be myself, a happy guy, and create a project, but there is nobody [about whom] I say, 'I want to be like this.'"

Humility, which kept coming up in the interviews, was in some instances connected with personal honesty. For Raimundo Morales of Banco de Crédito, you could be both humble and honestly proud. "You don't have to transmit to people that you're the best and the top," he explained, "but you can feel that you're the best of the top people." Just be humble in the way you convey that. "I think that's very, very important," he concluded.

Patience Is a Virtue

In business everyone seems to be in a hurry. Little hurries to get to work on time (or early), big hurries to beat your sales target, medium-size hurries to get everyone signed on to your goals. However, the executives I met regarded patience as an important quality for CEOs to have and cultivate. One experience has stuck with Lucas Chow, CEO of MediaCorp Singapore, when he worked at SingTel. Lucas was frustrated with the different speeds at which he and his peers were working; a colleague said to him, "Lucas, if you're riding in a car and people are still riding on elephants, you need to learn to wait for those to catch up." That advice has stuck with him. "It was a wake-up call," he told me. "You have to realize that you are where you are because you're moving at a pace that's much faster—if you are truly a leader, you're probably twenty paces ahead of everybody else. But you need to learn how to wait for those to catch up with you."

Todd Stitzer of Cadbury Schweppes echoed this sentiment. "I think emotional intelligence, patience, knowing yourself and how you impact others and how others impact a situation are all important," he said. "Reading people, reading a situation, listening before speaking—all those things are important."

François Barrault put it bluntly: "You need to like what you do. You need to like people. You need a good mix between ego and empathy. If you have too much ego, you do not take people with you. If you have too much empathy, you stay where you are."

He made another point that was, in its own way, exemplary: "I have learned to know myself. As an example, I am a very, very fast decision maker. But when I am tired, I say, 'Sorry, I am not good now, I will be better in two hours or tomorrow.'" He described it as closing "the decision machine, and you reopen it when you feel better."

Trust Others to Do the Job

Many of the CEOs I've met with over my years of experience as a recruiter agree that delegating is an essential art, and the ones I interviewed for this book stressed this as well. An almost bigger challenge is trusting those you've entrusted with the task. "I'm a big believer in division of labor," Terry Marks told me. "If I'm looking over your shoulder, doing your job all the time, it's because (a) I don't trust you or have confidence in you, or (b) I'm trying to demonstrate to you that I can roll up my sleeves. Well, that's all well and good, but that means something's not getting done. And it's just critical to surround yourself with highly capable people who can be trusted, have good judgment, and know when to bring issues to your attention, because that then frees you up to focus on areas in which you can add value."

Even the smartest, most skillful CEO has to rely on a lot of people. So get used to learning how to trust people and articulate properly what you want them to do. Clear instruction plus a trusting boss go a lot farther than doing something yourself because you feel you know exactly how you want it to be done. Ben Verwaayen gladly gives credit to others. "I think the best way to describe the success here is that I don't think that I'd made any decisions last month. Not a single one. I have a lot of other people to make the right decisions. That is very rewarding."

Of course you're going to be let down sometime because one CEO's delegation is another's dereliction of duty, and one team member's responsibility is another's overloading. Steve Shindler learned this the hard way. "My first boss in banking was very much an in-your-face kind of guy and helped to make sure that I knew what my priority was each day and he would peer in the doorway and say, 'You've got to get these things done today.' The next boss that I had in the bank was completely the opposite—he was very laid-back and it was up to me to figure out how to allocate my time. Then I came to a time in my career when I was ready to build my own portfolio, and one guy tells me I didn't know how to delegate enough, and then five years later the review is that you're delegating too much, and you've got to get back in." The lesson here is to not only to ensure delegation but to manage expectation, and match the delegation with a qualified recipient.

"A good CEO sets the stage and allows other people to make the right decisions," Ben Verwaayen said. "The idea that you can sit here and change the world is not true. There are limitations to what you can do."

We have all had bad experiences when we have given someone a task and let them get on with it and then been disappointed when they failed to deliver what we expected. Delegating and trust cannot be a one-way thing, with you giving and everyone else either fulfilling your trust or failing. In the end it is about opening up, knowing others and letting them know you more, and then putting your faith in one another. In a way, this kind of success requires compassion, the ability to really understand and empathize with people's experiences. On this subject, Steve Reinemund quoted his onetime boss, the late Wayne Calloway, who said, "If people don't think you care, they don't really care what you think."

Be Decisive

When Barack Obama and Hillary Clinton went head-to-head in a Democratic Party presidential candidate debate in January 2008, one of the issues that separated them and that the Clinton side had played up a lot was her experience. She could hit the ground running, they said. She would be able to make decisions from "day one" in the Oval Office. Obama came back with one of the most telling comments of the night: "Senator Clinton, I think, fairly, has claimed that she's got the experience on day one. And part of the argument that I'm making in this campaign is that it is important to be right on day one."

So, are you good at making the right decisions? Well, since you're not running for chief executive of the nation, you can afford to be a little less hard on yourself. You will make many decisions. Some will be right, some will be wrong, some you might never know, no matter how many times you play them over in your head. But the message from the executives I spoke to is this: while of course you always try to make the right decision, and you should never be hasty or ignore the evidence, the most important thing is to decide.

Bob Reynolds called upon his experience as a part-time college football referee (Reynolds was also short-listed to become commissioner of the National Football League) when drawing parallels with the decisions he's had to make in the corner office. "You have to think fast on your feet and you learn how to handle tough situations [without getting] ruffled. The coaches are uptight, the fans are uptight, the players are uptight, and they're looking for you to say, 'Okay. Here's what happened. Here's the play.' And make the decision and go. It helped me take tough situations and say, 'Okay. What've we got?'" Of course, Reynolds has fifteen years of referee experience that helped sharpen his ability to decide things on the spot, but you can still take his philosophy to heart. "If it seems insurmountable break it up in smaller pieces, and then it becomes not insurmountable," he said. Understand that you'll never make a perfect decision. "Make a decision and go and don't look back. You [can't say], 'Let me go check the book and I'll get back to you.'"

Like Reynolds, Steve Shindler insisted that learning to make a call is part of what sets CEOs apart. He recalled a lesson he learned from his first supervisor at Nextel, who was blunt but honest with him about the daunting tasks that lay ahead. "My first boss was Dan Ackerson, and he said, 'This is a company that was a hodgepodge, a variety of small companies coming from all over the place. You're going to spend the first six months turning over a lot of rocks. And underneath you're going to find a lot of snakes. The best advice I can give you is don't pile up those snakes into a corner and wait to make decisions. Make the decisions. Know that you have enough confidence in yourself, and intelligence in yourself, that you're going to make ninety percent of them correctly. And you're also going to know that ten percent of them are wrong. And you're going to go back and you'll recognize that within a reasonable period of time and you'll fix those ten percent rather than building a pile of things that get so big and so deep that you're knee-deep in it for the rest of your career trying to dig yourself out and nothing ever moves forward.'"

The third element of Reinemund's leadership model—the hands—is a bit like this. "At the end of the day you got to get it done," he said. "And people have to understand how to get things done and how to prioritize on the run, and be pragmatic. Great leaders that I've seen always have a Plan A, a Plan B, a Plan C, a Plan D, and they don't keep going down the road to Plan A when it's obvious that they need a Plan B."

CMGI's Steven Crane said he thought a leader is someone who is focused on leadership, knowing what you've got to do and that it's you who has to do it, then doing it and getting on with the next job. "At the end of the day you have to make hard decisions," he told me, "and there's got to be a decision maker. I think it's a talent to be able to say, yeah, I hear everything everybody is saying, but this is where we're going. And everybody steps in behind."

Just as Ackerson advised Shindler to trust that he will be right most of the time, Ben Verwaayen advised, "Trust your gut feeling. Many people think you can calculate everything. Dimension is so important. If you can't trust your gut feel you're probably not the right person or not the right material."

François Barrault called this intuition. It came up several times in our interview. He was not only unapologetic about his belief in a leader's quick-fire judgment, but thought too many executives did not exercise nearly enough of it. "I will give you an example," he said, and told of how he hired a "very senior guy in the U.S." who flew from Dallas to Barrault's summer home in Brittany on the French coast to be interviewed for the job. "So, I book a room in a hotel. The guy [came] into the room. After ten seconds I was ninety percent positive; after three minutes it was done. So, I say to myself, shit, this guy [came all this way] so I need to spend time with him, but the decision was done."

This was not about agonizing hours of interviews and character appraisals, nor even about painstaking executive search procedures, alas. On the contrary, the way he told it, it could have been a young rocker deciding whom to choose to play bass guitar in the band. But for Barrault, with all those years of experience behind him, it was not only important to listen to the voice within him. More than that, he thought it was something not enough leaders do: "You know, many CEOs are afraid of their soul, their heart, and whatever and they should not [be], because there is a lot of richness in listening to the emotions, intuition of people. I think good leaders today are people who are sensitive and learn and listen to their emotions because they can capture the essence of life, which is the sense of your business, your customers and the employers and what the energy is, what the vibe is."

It is this ability to almost intuitively grasp the meaning of the moment that can make the difference. CTPartners' Brian Sullivan maintained that a talent for pulling together the wider and long-term implications of many small lessons—and then being able to convey them clearly to others—was one of the most important things an executive search firm looked for in a candidate: "The ability to articulate the past, the present, and the future. What worked, what didn't, and what they did about it. It's important to understand how they [executive candidates] think, not just what they thought. As an executive progresses they rely less on their technical acumen and more on their ability to influence and, as a result, lead. Being able to make sense in a clear concise fashion is a key component for leadership."

Don't Get Derailed by Failure

Like many of the other executives I spoke to, Javier Gutiérrez of Ecopetrol saw the most common causes of failure as: putting personal interests before company ones; not having a long-term strategic vision of the company; and acting in what he called "an isolated way"—poor teamwork. But, like pretty much everyone, Gutiérrez stressed the need to learn from mistakes, indeed to see them as opportunities. It is important to "manage failure with transparency," as he put it.

In other words, don't let failure get you down. Indeed, the ability to shake it off and move on is what matters in the C-suite. "Of course you make mistakes, plenty of mistakes," Ben Verwaayen told me in his typical straightforward fashion. "Admit them, learn from it, move on. Don't cry over them."

Walt Bettinger understood the knee-jerk reaction to failure and described to me how he deals with it. "It can be easy to wrap ourselves up in the failure rather than saying the failure is an event and can be overcome," he said. "But some people are good at forgiving others and are lousy at forgiving themselves. Some people are really good at forgiving themselves, and have a hard time forgiving others. I think one of the lessons learned along the way is we have to be able to do both. So when we fail, we have to say, 'I failed but I'm not a failure. Or, you failed in this case, but you are not a failure.'"

Better yet, turn the failure into a lesson.

For Raimundo Morales of Banco de Crédito, not only should you own up to your mistakes pretty quickly ("Don't let your superiors find out about it afterwards," he warned), but you should make it instantly clear that you are going to work out what went wrong ("Reconstruct what happened")—and put it right. He wants to hear you say, "Look, I made this mistake and this is the way I'm going to correct it."

Bill Nuti of NCR said failures "taught me great, great lessons. I think one's scar tissue tells me a lot about your ability to be successful in the future. I think you have to have some scar tissue."

Meanwhile, if your failure gets you fired, here's some advice from Brian Sullivan on how to react: "You need perspective. In some ways, it's like getting divorced. We all have friends who have been divorced and we don't think any less of the husband or wife because of it. It's simply not a big deal . . . until it happens to you. Dust yourself off, figure out what really happened, and move forward."

Morales had a similar view: "The best thing for somebody being fired is that they should take an objective look as to why they are being fired rather than trying to justify themselves and assuming the person firing them is really making a mistake." Most often people are fired because they are in the wrong job, he said, not because there is something wrong with their ability. He knew of many cases where people were not suited to being an executive or a banker and they left and made a success of some other career, usually in private business.

Don't Sit in the Easy Chair

You might be tempted once you get to the top not to want to do anything that will invite failure. Play it safe. Challenges? Who needs any more? You had plenty on the way up, right? François Barrault was firm about this when we spoke. "My strong advice is don't stay in your comfort zone," he said. "I've run a marathon. It was uncomfortable, but I did it. When I chose to be in business, I had five options. Four were easy, in my comfort zone, but I took the toughest one." When I asked Barrault specifically what aspiring C-suiters should do, he didn't just talk about taking risks in the boardroom. "It is important to travel, to go to other countries, to discover different systems, and I think not to be afraid to do very painful things that are different," he told me. With this idea as with many of the others outlined in this book, many great CEOs extend the attitudes and qualities that make them successful as executives to their personal lives, ensuring an overall rich, fulfilling life that isn't just limited to the office.

"My definition of fun is to see people do things they thought they were never able to," Ben Verwaayen said. He recalled an instance earlier in his career. "Somebody said to me, 'Don't go to Lucent because they'll never accept you.' People have [said that about] almost all of my jobs. But to go through change, and to do the extraordinary different thing is what I like to do."

A risk-taking attitude will help you reach your full potential. In a practical sense, this kind of career adventurousness will help you get there, because those above you will notice you're always striving to do more and be better at what you do. Ron Williams sees junior people who don't want to take risks as people who also don't want to take leaps in their careers. The real test comes when a business is on fire, when jumping in to help put it out would be a high risk. "Those people who want to take [an] incremental step aren't interested in a business that's on fire," Williams said. "They want to go to the place that's safe and predictable and where it's a very logical next step up."

In fact, many a corporate chief is, in his first months, a fire chief. Rick Dreiling told me this story about when he took over Duane Reade: "I remember calling [my wife] after the first ten days saying, 'Oh, my God. Oh, my God. Do you realize what I've done?' And she said to me, which is probably the greatest advice I can give to these kids, you know, 'They wouldn't have replaced the old guy if everything was rosy.'

"If you sit back and think about it, that's right. So the first thing I would say is you're probably in that chair, great if everything's great and the CEO's just retired. But if you think about it in this day and age, not a lot of CEOs retire in the chair anymore."

Jim Donald's Seven Steps to Success

The executives I spoke to for this book covered considerable management territory, addressing my many questions about what it takes to do their jobs and generously offering insights and lessons beyond those. As you have seen, I have taken what they've said and grouped it according to subject areas—a bit from this person on that point, a bit from that person on another. I have made one exception, and that is on what former Starbucks CEO Jim Donald calls his "Seven Steps to Success." There is an unfolding logic and narrative in what Donald outlined in his interview with me, and I felt it best to allow it to remain intact.

Step 1. Go where you've never been before. "So I'm out in warehouses where no CEOs have been, on the midnight stocking crew. I'm everywhere. And what I found was amazing to me what people thought a CEO should be and what a CEO really is. You see, to lead a company, to really lead a company, you can't lead 'em from the C-suite. You've gotta lead 'em from the floor. You've gotta lead 'em from the warehouse; you've gotta lead 'em from the back room; you gotta lead 'em from the boardroom. And until you have buy-in from not just your executives but all the employees in one particular company, you're not gonna move the company forward." Unfortunately, too many CEOs get mired in strategy formulation and public relations. It is easy to get snared by this and spend every waking moment isolated from the people who really matter. When you study CEOs who get fired, the most common reason is that they were unaware of problems on the front line since they relied on second- and thirdhand information. An invisible leader usually becomes completely invisible soon.

Step 2. Communicate to everybody in the organization. "Pathmark [a regional supermarket chain that Donald turned around from bankruptcy after his time at Wal-Mart] had eleven years of declining same-store sales, eleven years when I took it over. I did a video and it said, 'We're a sick company right now.' And I said, 'This company is gonna go down, and we'll all be out of work,' and I showed 'em the numbers. I showed 'em the forty-four quarters of declining comps, I showed 'em the interest rate on the debt was higher than the [earnings]. And what was funny about this in my first two months of travels was that because Pathmark was such a high-volume store, they didn't know. These unionized employees were never told what the heck was going on. So I sent this video out, made it mandatory, and I paid them to watch this. That was the turnaround of this company. When the employees on the front line knew what the problem was, we just simply turned it over to them and said, 'Help us fix it.'

"They hated management, and management never came out of their offices to see what the heck was going on. My first day on the job was in Newark, New Jersey, at one-thirty in the morning. That's when I started: one-thirty in the morning. And I walk up to this stocker and I say, 'Hey, how're you doing?' You know what he told me? He goes, 'What the fuck is it to you?' I said, 'Well, it's a lot to me. I'm your new president.' And he goes, 'President of what?' I said, 'President of Pathmark.' He goes, 'Shit. They never tell me anything that's going on.'" In the absence of communication, rank-and-file employees have a way of seeing facts from their perspective that could be detrimental to you and your organization. Whether the news is good or bad, they appreciate candor and continued communication. The resentment that stems from lack of communication can destroy an organization.

Step 3. Have a fish story. "In the first two or three months as I was going around, we were still in the doldrums. Negative same-store sales still existed, so I called a breakfast meeting. I had about eighteen hundred people at this meeting in New Jersey. I had vendors, manufacturers, I had managers, and so I'm talking about the state of this company. And I pull this fresh salmon out of this Styrofoam ice chest, and I said, 'This is the kind of company I want to be.' And I held this fish up, and I said, 'I want to be the fish like the salmon that swims upstream when others are coming down, meaning that if we can catch our competition resting on their laurels as we make our way upstream, we'll end up winning.' And I said, 'I want to be the fish that jumps over these hurdles and obstacles called debt that get in the way, you know, like a salmon jumps over stones and boulders.' But I said, 'This is what I want to become, and I want to become like this salmon.' People liked it; they could associate the turnaround of Pathmark with this fish.

"And you can imagine, I took this fish with me everywhere I went. When we went to borrow $500 million at the Waldorf my CFO said, 'No. Don't bring the fish.' I said, 'I'm bringing the fish.' Well, we got the $500 million [we were seeking], and this is where the 'Have a fish story' comes into play. Three years later we're going back to the Waldorf, because now the company's public, and we're having our first meeting with investors, and I go back to the AV technician and said, 'Here's my presentation if you want to load this up.' He goes, 'Pathmark, huh?' I said, 'Yeah.' He said, 'You should have been here three years ago. They had this crazy CEO waving this fish around.' And I said, 'That was me, you fool!' But he remembered that.

"So when I talk to students, when I talk to employees, [I ask] what [have you got that will] leave an impression with a customer, with somebody you're interviewing, or with a professor? What is *your* fish story? What is that story that they'll always remember?" When my current boss, Brian Sullivan, chairman of CTPartners, took on his role, I remember his wife, Pam, telling him, "Sully, you didn't need any new stories. You just needed a new audience." Sullivan is a master at using the same story repeatedly with different audiences, always capturing their attention. It is a trait that comes naturally to some but it is one that can be learned. Use your USP (unique selling proposition) and use it to your advantage. People will remember you for it.

Step 4. Encourage risk taking with the freedom to fail. "Basically, Pathmark was turned around, not because of me, but because we enabled our store associates the opportunity to take risk. And here's where it all started. I walk into a Delaware store, and I meet this seafood manager. His name is Nelson. And I said, 'Hey, how's business?' He goes, 'It sucks.' These Pathmark associates could really tell you what's on their mind. And I said, 'Well, what do you mean?' He said, 'Because you and all your friends at the corporate office tell me what to sell, and I know what to sell.' I said, 'Well, give me an example.'

"He takes me over to the seafood counter and all this stuff we shipped in. Now, he's in Delaware; he's not in New York. And what they sold in Delaware didn't necessarily sell in New York, and vice versa. I said, 'So what do you want to sell?' He said, 'Redfish are running right now.' I said, 'So order in fifty pounds.' He goes, 'There's no way.' I said, 'I like your style. Order in a hundred pounds.' He goes, 'I'll get fired.' I said, 'Order in three hundred pounds, and you sell it.' He sold it within two days."

Around the same time, said Donald, he came across a saying attributed to James Bryant Conant, onetime president of Harvard, "that a turtle only moves forward when it sticks his neck out. So I came up with this award, which was a turtle with the Pathmark logo. And when employees would go out of their way, take a risk on selling items, providing service or cutting expenses, they would win this turtle award. And the week I left Pathmark, the turtle award was annualizing at $100 million of revenue, which is $20 million of [earnings]." Numerous books address the risk-reward scenario, but it never ceases to amaze me how CEOs who take amazing risks themselves are unwilling to let others take them. If you do not let your employees take risks you have one of two problems—you haven't learned how to effectively manage your team yet or you have B- and C-players on your team who have not earned your confidence. Get A-players and give them the freedom to fail if you wish to succeed.

Step 5. Never be bigger than the front line. This is the lesson Donald was taught so vividly by Sam Walton, founder of Wal-Mart, at the beginning of this chapter.

Step 6. To change the culture, you have to change the language. This was Donald's way of saying, Listen more. "CEOs sometimes think they have to know all the answers, and they don't. And to change this particular culture of any company, if one would start listening and doing more of that than preaching or talking, they'll find that the entire culture of the company changes. Because people will say, 'Hey, he or she cares about what I say.' And that will make them start thinking about ideas and suggestions and things."

Step 7. Celebrate the success of others. For Donald, one story explains this principle in all its glory: "I'm in a board meeting at Pathmark, and my assistant comes in and says, 'Jack's on the phone.' Well, Jack's my stepfather. Well, I don't even take calls from anybody when I'm in a board meeting because it's a board meeting. And I said, 'Look, tell him I'll call him back.' She goes, 'No, you need to talk to him.' I'm looking at her. I'm saying, 'Tell him

I'll call him back.' She goes, 'No, you need to talk to him.' So I'm having this argument with my assistant in front of my board. The board says, 'Go talk to him. Quit being such an asshole.'

"So I go in there to my office, she steps inside my office, she shuts my door, and she's looking at me talking to my stepfather, Jack, who's eighty years old. And I get on the phone, and he can't even speak. He's just like, he's like going, 'Jimmy.' And ... and I said, 'Jack, what's wrong? Is something wrong with Mom?' My mom was seventy-nine. He goes, 'Jimmy, Jimmy.' I said, 'Jack, what is it, what is it?' And he kept going on and on. I finally said, 'Jack, tell me what's going on.'

"He goes, 'I shot my age today!' I said, 'What?' He goes, 'I shot a 79 on the golf course.' I said, 'Jack, I'm in the middle of this board meeting,' and I looked at my assistant, and she said, 'Hey, Mister Big Shot, why don't you take a little bit of time to celebrate this success. You don't know how long Jack's gonna be around. Take five minutes.' And she slams the door, and she held the door so I couldn't come out.

"Well, it's a huge lesson there. It meant the world to Jack. So now I'm in Florida a year later talking to six hundred sales executives for the Wrigley Gum Company. My mom and my stepdad live in Florida. They're in the front row. I'm telling 'em this seventh step. So after these talks people usually come up to see me, you know, and talk to me. They all went over to Jack. And to this day he still gets Wrigley gum golf balls, tees, towels, and all this stuff."

Moral of the story? "If one would take the time to celebrate the success of people at every level of the organization, all you're doing is throwing another log onto the fire. You are just continuing to fuel the energy, whether it's Luis, the guy that cleans your office at night, or whether it's your executive vice president. Everybody needs their success celebrated. You've gotta worry about the success of others no matter how small it is."

Donald said he was thinking of writing up his Seven Steps to Success into a book. I can't wait.

Executive Summary

It's all right to want to be the best. If all your life you've striven for the top, that's a good start. But that alone will not get you there. Because to be the best CEO, you need a range of talents and skills to lead, communicate, and inspire, without which you cannot win anyway.

Listen to the moral tales of your childhood. When you are faced with ethical and personal choices, the best voices to pay heed to will be the ones that echo from your childhood. They will ensure that you embrace the qualities you will need—integrity, selflessness, judgment, keeping your word, and, most important, knowing right from wrong.

You are not number one. The company is. So think of yourself as being there to serve, not just the shareholders who will expect you to do so, but your employees and your customers. Patience is a quality that will go a long way in dealing with all of them.

Use your head. The C-suite is no place for smart-asses or know-it-alls. You need to be intelligent and thoughtful. That means admitting the gaps in your knowledge and experience and building a team and structures to fill them. Be true to yourself: while you should be humble in your dealings with others, it is all right to feel proud of what you've done.

Delegate, delegate, delegate. It is a mistake to try to do too much yourself or to look over everyone's shoulder. You'll never get anything done and you'll only irritate your team. But to delegate, you first have to build trust with those who will do the work because you won't be able to do so if you don't have faith in one another.

Wrong is okay, but indecisive is not. You do not always have to be right, but you do always have to make a decision. Don't be impulsive and ignore the signs, but do listen to your intuition and make a judgment. Prevarication is the thief of credibility.

Turn failure into opportunity. Don't be afraid of mistakes. Avoid them until you've made them, but then examine them closely so you can find out what went wrong. And then set them right. And never wait for someone else to point them out when you know you've made a mistake.

Look for new challenges. It is tempting to take the easy option and avoid anything risky or adventurous, but down that road lurks stagnation and complacency. Comfortable is careless.

Chapter 9

How's Your Day Been?

L et's say you've done it all—built up your experience, surrounded yourself with team players, found mentors, did the right net-working. Thanks to the insights of the executives we have met, we know what kind of person it takes to be a true leader, and which values to cultivate throughout your career journey. But now that you're finally in your corner office, what's this job all about?

This is how Todd Stitzer of Cadbury Schweppes explained it: "I describe it as standing in front of a fire hydrant with your mouth open. I don't think the most enthusiastic and driven of people are quite ready for the experience. You have just enough time to breathe, but not very much. You have to prepare yourself for that. You have to know that it's going to happen, and you have to make sure that you have people helping you sort out and synthesize. And you have to pick your spots to prioritize where you apply your energy and in-sight because it will end up being a twenty-four-and-a-half-hour-a-day job."

Of course, it's not going to be like this every day. Just nearly every day. And the days that might be the worst are often the ones when you were thinking you might be able to sit back a bit and reflect or read that *Harvard Business Review* article someone said you really ought to look at. It's not just the relentlessness of the pressure from the fire hydrant: it's never being sure when the thing is going to go off.

"I enjoy the glory, the power, and so on—that is the beautiful part—but the responsibility of the job outweighs all of this glory," Goh Sik Ngee of Yellowpages.com admitted. "I think that the influence of a CEO over the life of the people in the organization, and shareholders, is much more than what I imagined in my particular job. My company has hundreds of people [in it]. So if they each have their own family, let's say three or four dependents—those are thousands of people's lives [that] to a large extent depend on you. And if you make a wrong decision and you do the wrong thing, a thousand or more people's lives will be affected as a result. Of course, on the other hand, if [the company] does do good, then people do benefit. That's not something that was obvious to me when I was one of a thousand or more people and not a CEO."

And while people like Goh live and breathe that obligation daily, your employees will remind you, too. "I'm going to state the obvious: you're going to work harder than you ever worked in your life," Russ Fradin of Hewitt told me. And part of that work includes the requests he gets on his lunch break when he goes down to the company cafeteria and people from all departments in the company approach him with complaints. "They expect you to fix it—and it's a reasonable expectation." For them, yes. But you might need to slip away occasionally and remind yourself of the relative importance of the issues to them vis-à-vis you, because often it isn't going to feel that important to you. You're trying to have lunch, for heaven's sake, but you can't forget that the buck stops at you.

Ron Williams of Aetna expects every day to be full of problems—but with the right approach, he can manage it. "For me, it's not a question of 'Is there a problem?' The question every day is, 'What is the nature of the problem?' " he said. "And once you shift from 'Will there be problems?' to the nature of the problems, then you get out of the [attitude] of 'Why is the world picking on us, or me?' That is the way of the world. There is *always* a problem. But what are we going to do about it; are we solving it the right way, are we approaching it from a values-based perspective, are we articulating our vision in a way that we are trying to solve it?" Very mature. But Williams is a mature man and an experienced executive. Lesser mortals take a long time getting over the instinctive reaction of feeling self-pity and despair when something goes wrong. And even when you've gotten over that, it is often difficult not to be thinking impatiently, *And what is it this time?* Getting from there to the Williams method of welcoming and dealing with problems takes all the human resilience and mental courage that separates real leaders from the rest.

One of the most galling frustrations executives complained about was regulation. Some said it had gotten better in the last few years, but in the immediate post-Enron era it became unbearable for some. CMGI's Steven Crane told me this story: "I remember a few years ago, when it [the obsession with regulation] was at its peak, there was a CFO of one of the restaurant companies, very well regarded, they said. I remember he announced his resignation on a quarterly call. He just said, 'I'm tired of having people assume that I'm a criminal.' On the call. On the conference call. And I thought, 'Wow, good for him.' "

So, if they don't quit with a flourish like that, how do these top CEOs deal with the inevitable daily problems? John Swainson, for one, rebuilt a hobbled CA, Inc. by doing some serious retrenching, and Infosys Technologies' Nandan Nilekani sees his daily job as something like a futurologist's—making sure he gathers information to understand the future so he can make decisions now. Bill

Amelio of Lenovo likens his daily drill to keeping a drumroll going. Here is a peek into the day-to-day lives of the CEOs who run today's major companies.

Everyone's Your Boss

One of the biggest ironies when you get to the top is that suddenly everyone's your boss. As Russ Fradin and Goh Sik Ngee's little accounts of how this happens illustrate, you'll be reminded of that continually.

"You always think that when you get to the CEO job you don't have a boss. I hate to say it, but everybody is," Lee Hsien Yang told me, in a brutally frank way. "Everybody thinks they own you. The shareholders think they own you, the employees think they own you, the board thinks they own you, the regulators think they own you. You answer to everybody. You're not the boss. You're a slave to all of these people."

Javier Gutiérrez of Ecopetrol calls this the "relativeness of power," something good leaders have to learn. "There exist directions that must be followed, even if one doesn't agree with them," he explained.

As if it is not enough to be making concessions to those with accountable power themselves, you'll also be under media scrutiny. "I personally think having to deal with the media is one of the most unpleasant parts of a CEO job," Lee said. I asked him what you can do about it. "Well, you can go for media training, and you can learn to do it," he said matter-of-factly. "I think most people who work in management eventually know how to deal with interpersonal relationships. If you don't figure that out, then you're not going to get ahead." Ironically, the fact that we met in the Shangri-La Hotel in Singapore meant Lee attracted a lot of attention, given his elevated status in the small island nation. But he showed no signs of being distracted and gave me his full attention, evidence that he had figured it out a long time ago.

Indeed, if you begin to adjust yourself to this reality of the job—that everyone thinks they have a right to your time and your attention—you'll be a lot better off.

"Before I got to this position, I did not have as detailed an appreciation for the amount of time, effort, and energy that it would take to communicate with the financial community or shareholders," Todd Stitzer said. "As someone who grew up in a business—I've been at Cadbury Schweppes for twenty-five years—I was certainly aware of the dynamic, but I think until you get very close to the top you don't actually interface with them. And when you get to the top you have a crash course in getting up to speed on that subject, which can be energizing, interesting, and exciting. But it's something that I'm trying to share with my executive team, to give them some experience in going to shareholder meetings and road shows with me so they're ready for it when and if they get the chance."

Carl Bass of Autodesk also found that once he got to the top, he was far from the big boss that many people assume you are when you've got the title. "There is part of your job in which you work for the people who, by title or by organization structure, work for you," he said. "I think if somebody assumed when they got to the CEO job that this dynamic would change, it doesn't. In all levels of management you're often doing work on behalf of your employees, clearing roadblocks, clearing obstacles, fund-raising, mostly for the benefit of your organization. And the same continues to be true [for CEOs]."

Not Everyone Likes You

If you are already a manager of some sort, you've probably already figured out that one of the fallouts from the job is that you might not always win the popularity contest. In no walk of life does everyone love the person who makes the decisions. It's one of the constant sites of struggle in family life, whether it's bringing up children or sharing responsibility for a home with your spouse. Imagine that, for CEOs, multiplied many times over. This may especially be the case when you come in new to a company.

Lucas Chow of MediaCorp Group said this about being liked: "When you enter into a company, a new environment, or new organization, initially you would think that people would welcome you with open arms. But more often than not, there are always two groups of people. One group can easily identify with you, immediately can share with you the same kind of visions and values and so on. There's another group of people who will [think], 'Another new kid on the block. Let's see how he's going to deliver.' And you have yet another party that no matter what you do, they're never going to be convinced." So how do you combat that? Accept it, Chow said. "After I changed companies three times in various jobs, I started to realize that this is something I should anticipate," he told me. "And I shouldn't set my expectations too high. No matter how good your credentials are, when you take on a new job, your reputation doesn't come automatically. You are as good as your last job."

"Leadership is a contract," Sanjiv Ahuja of Orange told me, acknowledging in the same way as Chow that people have expectations of you that you have to take into account, however unreasonable or negative they might seem. But on the flip side, earning your employees' respect requires being a decisive, firm leader as well, even if they don't always like it. "You ask people what they expect of you and then you tell them what you expect of them. You make sure both sides are very clear. And then you tell your team [what] is critical to you and stick to it. You'd better expect that from anybody who is part of your team. You say cost is critical to you, schedule is critical, customer satisfaction is critical. Stand up for what you believe in, and then the team delivers."

As in many things, it's your record that counts. Even those who are skeptical of you and may be waiting for you to make your first mistake that will prove them right can come around if you make yourself plain: this is what I am here to do; this is what I expect of you to help achieve it; and this is how we're going to measure our success. Now let's get on with the job.

Know What's Going On

A number of CEOs mentioned that once they got to the top, the flow of information changed—it became harder to get certain pieces of information, and they had to be more strategic about it. "When you operate a business unit or even a regional unit, the information flow from your area or geographic or business responsibility is pretty significant, but when you become the chief executive, you become responsible for everyone's information flow," Todd Stitzer explained. "Being able to filter it, synthesize it, and then wield it to your benefit is something that is a constant responsibility. You have to stay on top of it, sort through it, use what you need most effectively. The information never stops. In a global business somebody's working almost all the time."

In your information gathering, it's more important than ever to keep information channels open, inside and outside of the company. On a daily basis you'll have to solve problems, and the more resources you have, the better. "The real challenge is understanding what the issues are that hold people back, what are the issues that hold companies back, and what do you do about those?" John Swainson of CA, Inc. said. "You have to get involved and start diagnosing what the issues are. Get an outside view of this company. What is its market potential? How is it perceived by its customers? Where is it going? What's its best path forward? And you have to have people who can tell you that, and often those are not people inside the firm. You need an outside-in perspective. You have some of that when you come into a firm, and you very rapidly lose it."

CTPartners' Brian Sullivan saw this as the "classic CEO failure"—when the chief becomes too far removed from the operations of the business. "All [through] their careers they move up because they know how to make money. Then for some reason they detach themselves from the business and people feel abandoned. People sign up for someone who understands how difficult it is to do business day-to-day and tries to help them. They will not last long working for someone who abandons them and morphs into a strategist. Want to be a strategist? Join McKinsey."

This proved to be one of the most difficult areas in which to find the right balance: detail versus big picture. At first it seemed like an either-or problem, but it became clear, as I spoke in more detail to each interviewee, that what they were saying was that the good executive is someone who, on the one hand, can appreciate the detail but feed it into the bigger picture while, on the other hand, not becoming so big-picture-focused that everyone else feels they're doing the work and the boss is looking over the rainbow.

François Barrault, already well established in my mind as someone who loves the counterintuitive and the unexpected, told me a story about a moment over dinner with some other executives when he was given an insight that illustrated the importance of plain good thinking. One of the guests was the chairman of Nestlé, and he asked, "François, who is my biggest competition now? Mars? Pepsi? Whatever?" And the answer was none of these. It was Barrault's own BT Global Services, he said. "Five years ago seventy percent of the pocket money of kids was to buy chocolates, ice cream; now eighty percent is in telecom. Do you think anybody in my team would have thought about that? Can you imagine the impact for my business?"

For Steven Crane, a similar thing came to mind when I asked him what needs to change as one moves from mid-level management to the C-suite. "I think the first thing that popped into my head is that the higher you go into the C-level organization, you've got to step back from the detail . . . and always pull back to look at the bigger picture. Every once in a while I've got to just step back and say, you know what, we're going to get through this, we will get through it. There's no question. So don't just get so wrapped up in the day-to-day stuff." And even when you are looking at the detail, said Crane, ask: "Is this consistent with the strategy, is it on strategy, are you doing the right things for the company?"

Crane, who is a qualified pilot, used an analogy from his experience of flying to illustrate the point: "One of the things they talk about in pilot training is situational awareness. And what that means in pilot lingo is that a small plane moving at two miles a minute is going to be twenty miles ahead in, like, no time at all. So you've got to be thinking, where's this thing going? If I suddenly fly into cloud cover, I'm hosed. Whereas fifteen minutes ago, if I'd thought about it and looked at the weather, I'd have said oh, okay, I've got to divert and go to another airway." At Pepsi, where Crane spent time in his early career, he said they called this ability to see ahead and to address practical matters in this way "executive maturity."

When you're "flying" a company, you have your work cut out for you just keeping it in the air without having to worry about looking up, down, and sideways. In a plane you have instruments that help you do that, but when it involves people, you can't rely on instruments. You have to look people in the eye and determine the problems for yourself.

"When you come into a leadership role," said Martin Homlish of SAP, "you need to manage three ways. You need to manage down, you need to manage up, and you need to manage across—and don't forget that. If you focus all your time on managing up, you may think you're making progress with the senior leaders in the organization, but you will not have any soldiers who are going to follow you up that hill and you won't have any colleagues who are going to stand next to you. If you spend only time managing down, the people next to you and the people above you will have no idea what it is you're doing and you won't be able to get things done in the corporate environment. So, it's a very, very key skill to learn—the balance of that."

But don't forget the detail. Bill Nuti couldn't stress this point enough: "Learning how to look at your company through the eyes of your facts and your data is extraordinarily important and getting comfortable with that is very important. I am personally a super-cruncher, a proud super-cruncher by nature. I very much am a fact-based, data-driven decision maker. I do use intuition, there's no question about it, I use intuition, and I'll certainly use other data points, but I love regression, I love randomization, I love trend analysis, because it's not the data, it's the information that you cull out of the data."

The Customer Comes First

No matter what industry you are in, or where you're located, the one priority executives stressed that you cannot let slip is customer service. "I am obsessed by customer service," said François Barrault, whom I interviewed over breakfast in a restaurant near Trafalgar Square in London. He told me an example of something he did in an expensive hotel restaurant. In his story, he asked for an espresso and was told that they don't serve espresso. Barrault pointed out that they had an espresso machine, and the waiter said, "It's complicated, and you'll have to pay for that." He asked to speak to the manager, who didn't come. Finally, Barrault went to the hotel office. "I said, 'Let me tell you one thing. I am obsessed by customer service. You run this hotel, which is part of a big chain. There are hundreds of people working very hard for customer satisfaction. Let me tell you how your system is screwed up.' I am so obsessed that every time I see something wrong at the end of the food chain, which is serving the customer, I always go and see the top boss and explain the situation."

But while Barrault isn't afraid to criticize, he's also open to being on the receiving end. "I would love for people to say this to me. Young guys always focus on strategy and details, and these need to be connected all of the time. You are as good as the service you deliver. You need to have the humility to dive deep. If you are a restaurant manager, you need to go to your restaurant. I run a huge machine, but I'm going to sit down with the customer-service guy and explain how it works."

John Kealey of iDirect said he believes that at whatever stage in a career one is at, providing value should always come first. "At the end of the day, you have to provide value for the customer," he said. "Just be patient and persistent, and you'll find your way through these things." One of the ways he ensures that this happens at his company is by creating customer service from the inside of his company and out—if his employees are happy, they are in a better place to make their customers happy. "One of the things we have here at iDirect is that the team works really well together. People really enjoy being part of the company," Kealey said. "With all its challenges there's going to be difficulties, but if they really enjoy it, it comes out in every interaction they have with the customer."

Corporate Culture Begins with You

All companies have cultures, and employees imbibe that culture as they work, often in subtle and subconscious ways, just as culture is passed on in families, tribes, and wider societies, and carried across borders and generations. When you're in the C-suite, and finally in the CEO chair, you are responsible for creating your corporate culture, cultivating it and living it. "You must be passionate towards creating a culture, and it can only come from the top," Kiran Mazumdar-Shaw of Biocon told me. "I can't say that I've got this culture homogenously spread across the organization, because it can never happen as you grow larger," she admitted. "And whether you like it or not, you're going to have a lot of politics creeping in, even though you would like to believe there is no politics, because people are competing."

I noticed one aspect of Mazumdar-Shaw's corporate culture in action. It is something that I believe makes a strong statement about your company, apart from its obvious practical value. When I arrived at the company's offices, I was met by a striking woman who I thought must be Mazumdar-Shaw, whom I had never met personally before. I soon discovered, however, that it was Susan Kumar, her executive assistant. The quality of her interaction and intelligence of her conversation while we waited (briefly) for the boss reminded me of how important someone like this is to the executive who cares about everything. My own EA, Milagro Petty, sprang immediately to mind, with her strong work ethic and commitment.

John Kealey said that to keep his customers happy, he tries to keep his employees happy. It is all part of corporate culture, and to adhere to it he has instituted a five-value system that articulates that culture: be teamwork focused, customer focused, and revenue focused; have a passion to win; and keep your commitments. "What happens is people care a lot about the company and they care about their customers as a result. You get there by creating a place that people really want to be a part of. We've had very little turnover rate over the last five years and I think it's because people really like being here."

Steve Shindler of NII also prizes corporate culture highly. "We've built this business on a culture where we hold ourselves to the highest standards of ethics and integrity," he said. "We want to do the right thing all the time. We don't want people hiding things or not being transparent."

Your own behavior also counts, because it trickles down. "If you are the CEO of a company, you are the leader, and if you show that you have pain, the entire organization will feel that pain," Lucas Chow said. "If you sneeze, the organization worries whether you will catch a cold. Many times, sacrifice is necessary not just in terms of your personal time, but things like [showing your] emotions. It may not be advisable to show your true emotions all the time. You may be suffering, but you have to swallow your tears and cry silently."

Trial by Fire

As Todd Stitzer said so plainly, there is nothing that can prepare you for the pressures of being a CEO, and many of the executives I spoke to admitted that they learn by doing. "You have to be in the field, in the middle of the situation, and then you've got to figure out what to do about it," John Swainson said. "And it's not always easy to do that when you've got stuff flying in every direction.

"Road maps for doing this, and most of the hints-and-tips kinds of books on how to be an effective CEO, are, at best, very insufficient in terms of providing you with the ammunition you need to really do the job," Swainson continued. "They attempt to formulate an approach, and certainly there is wisdom in the approaches they prescribe, but I think it's different for every company and situation. There are vast differences in the situation that happened to any of the peers who I've talked to over the years."

So you are warned. And that's the point of the whole exercise: you cannot learn your executive management principles by heart (or keep *Management for Dummies* in your briefcase) and hope to get by. But prepare yourself as much as you can, and take the advice of the people who are already there—expect the unexpected.

As Jim Donald put it, "You have about a five-minute honeymoon period, okay? And that's when you sign a letter of agreement to become the CEO, because once you do, no matter what's happened in the past, you're at fault. And you gotta have thick skin and broad shoulders, and be able to articulate a strategy to get the business back on track, whether it's right or it's wrong."

Some executives warned that often it is the wider policy and regulatory environment that you did not prepare for—or you did prepare for it, but it changed rapidly while you were in charge. Arthur Collins found this one of the most striking changes during his time at the top of Medtronic: "how I spent my time even when I moved into this role early in 2001 and the amount of time that now is spent on activities that are outside of Medtronic but influence Medtronic, whether it be on policies that affect how our industry is regulated, or policies that affect how our products are reimbursed, issues that affect the legal environment in which we operate. And these are issues not just in the United States but outside the United States. And I think particularly for a CEO of a company that is an industry leader, it's the role not just that they play for their company but it is the role that they also play for the industry. Because many times decisions that are taken outside the company can have every bit as important an influence on the success of the company [as] those decisions that you take inside the company. I am spending more time on those issues than I would have predicted whether it be ten years ago or seven years ago."

When Bill Nuti, chairman and CEO of NCR Corporation, talked about the shock of the job, he emphasized the necessity of having a passion for your work to get you through. The regulatory environment was part of the challenge: "The thing people don't know about this job, particularly in our country, is that it's gotten far more difficult and far more risky over the last several years. And I'm not suggesting CEOs in the past had it easier, that's not my point. But the role of the CEO has become the role of the COO over time. The risks that we inherit in this job based on the experiences of Enron and WorldCom and others have gone up precipitously. The regulatory environment, with Sarbanes-Oxley, has become more challenging. And running a company in an ever-increasingly competitive world, where everything is getting cheaper faster forever, is not easy."

And then there are the ups and downs of the wider market and economy. Steve Shindler told me a story that couldn't illustrate better the pressures of the job. "It was early 2001 when the bubble burst, and here we were traveling the globe for four straight weeks while the Dow dropped an average of a hundred points a day," he recalled. "But we got through that, and we tried to figure out a plan. Nextel, our parent company at the time, had provided us with a term sheet for $250 million of additional funding that would have carried us quite a long way, but it had a lot of tough terms attached to it. The bondholders at the same time were looking at that term sheet saying they weren't prepared to agree to those terms. We certainly weren't

thrilled about a number of them, and the term sheet kind of lin-
gered for some period of time, and one day we found that Nextel
announced publicly that they were pulling that term sheet away from
us. They were taking away the commitment. I think it was a Wednesday morning that the press release hit, the people around here in
our headquarters group knew that that was our source of funding,
and it was obvious on people's faces that they thought that was the
end."

Now, the easy way out here would have been avoidance, and for a
CEO it would've been all too easy to disappear into his corner office
and wait for the news to hit by any other route than from him. But
Shindler gathered everyone into a conference room. When you meet
him, one of the first things that strikes you about Shindler is his energy. He's experienced, direct, and has a sense of humor. "I walked
into that room," he said, picking up the story, "and there were like
150 people in there that day. It was pretty much silent, but I walked
in with half [of them] expecting that I was going to come in and tell
them all to pack their bags and go home. And I said, 'Well, some of
you may have seen a press release that came out this morning, and
Nextel has pulled their commitment.' And then I asked a question. I
said, 'Are any of you in here nervous or worried?' There was no response. I said, 'I'm not. And let me tell you why.' And I looked every
single person in the eye and took a full minute and a half to look
around the room, and I said, 'For these reasons: the people we had
in the markets, the networks that we built, the kind of subscribers
that we had, the assets that we have, the spectrum position, all of the
things that we had lined up and built, they were still there.' [I said] I
was going to take it upon myself . . . to figure a way out of this.

"Now, I didn't know for sure, at that particular juncture, if that
would be possible. But I took it upon myself and then I brought my
team together, the general counsel, CFO, and a couple of other folks,

who said you know what, it's not only for the 150 people who were in this room, here in Reston, Virginia, that day. They're in the United States, and if this company goes under, they're all going to land somewhere and they're going to be absolutely fine. But we've got 3,500 people in markets that are in disarray in Argentina, which was in a meltdown, and Brazil, which was in utter chaos at the time, [in] Mexico, and [in] economies that were really struggling that represent 3,500 families. If we let this business go under, they won't be able to put food on the table for those families and for those kids for who knows how long, if ever again. So we are going to do everything and anything that we possibly can to get through this. And ultimately, we got some bondholders and they helped us with a term sheet and the rights offering and we pulled the whole thing together and did the prepackage and came through the bankruptcy."

A year later, Shindler walked into the same conference room, right after sending out an e-mail announcing that the bankruptcy court had approved the reorganization—and got a three-minute standing ovation. When he told me that story, it gave me goose bumps, and recalling it today, it still amazes me. Not a lot can prepare you for that sort of thing—it just comes with the job.

Lead the Troops

Being ready for whatever comes your way is good advice, but while you are doing that, there is the day-to-day to think about. A CEO's job is to create the workplace rhythm, and to keep it going. "[Leaders] know how to rally the troops and motivate people," Bob Reynolds of Fidelity told me. Steve Reinemund likened it to the military. "The principles are exactly the same. In any company, any organization where you're having to influence people to accomplish a task, it's exactly the same," he said. "A lot of people have a misconception of what the military is all about. They think it's about giving orders, but it isn't. I would say you have to be even more skilled to be an effective military leader than in business because the stakes are so high. You're talking about people's lives. But to get those young soldiers to go out and put their lives in harm's way every day doesn't happen by barking out a bunch of orders, because people are just not going to do that."

Nor is inspiring your troops merely a question of rank or courage. There are maps to read, radar signals to interpret, intelligence to be gathered. "It's not just a shoot-first-aim-later kind of thing," Nandan Nilekani of Infosys told me. "Certainly instinct and intuition are very important. At the end of the day, you're making a call, a judgment call. But I believe that today the information is at your disposal, if you can really harness it and develop insights from it, giving you a far more robust platform. And then you need to move."

"There's so many times when you have to make those snap judgment calls, and then you second-guess yourself," Steve Shindler told me. "In hindsight those ten percent of the decisions were a mistake. People who you would have wanted to go get or you wanted to retain or you lost, or you didn't get rid of soon enough. [Times when] you didn't take action and you probably could have made the company better as a result of just going with your gut feeling."

Indeed, a big part of the job has nothing to do with glamour and everything to do with clear strategy, clear tactics, and never forgetting about what you need to go into battle with, like cooks and medics as well as the guys with the guns. Bill Amelio put it this way: "The executives have to have the ability to be an operator, somebody who knows how to execute. *Executing* means to put a business management system in place, understand review cycles, and how to make sure an organization delivers consistent results that are in synch with

strategy. Good executives have to be both great strategists and execu-
tors. If you don't have a good execution bent, it's surprising how
quickly an organization can start to meander."

Amelio gave me an example: When AlliedSignal merged with
Honeywell in 1999, the deal brought together two CEOs, Lawrence
Bossidy of AlliedSignal and Michael Bonsignore of Honeywell. Bossidy became chairman of the new company and Bonsignore the
CEO. "Larry was an execution [person]. He focused on the quarter,
on operations, on checking in with all the business units, and identifying problems and opportunities as they emerged," Amelio explained. "The tides shifted dramatically when Michael Bonsignore
came in because he wanted to focus on growth, but was less focused
on quarterly execution. He started this concept of a growth task
force, and it meant that some of the most talented people in the organization had to work on a lot of different projects and priorities.
Nobody was doing the execution anymore. Then you started to see
one quarter get a little wobbly. Then things became more unstable.
Then things would really derail, because the focus on execution
wasn't there. It didn't take long to see what happens when people
lose focus on execution."

How do you avoid the wobbling? It's a difficult balance, and even
as Amelio explained it to me step by step, describing it as being like
delicately placed dominoes, it had a dizzying effect that really drove
home how important it is for a CEO to keep everything under control: "If you have people who aren't steeped in operations and steeped
in execution-bound thinking, then they'll lose focus and become
distracted by whatever seems to be the next thing as opposed to doing the most important things. People have to have the courage to
say, 'No, we're running a P and L.' If you want to run a P and L, you
have to have a certain set of skills to be able to pull that off and do it
successfully," Amelio said. "That means making sure everyone does

what they say they will do, and what they are supposed to do. You might ask, 'Well, isn't that what managers do?' Well, it is what your managers should be doing, but somewhere along the way, someone's got to coach them to think operationally, and to think about execution. Every organization has people who don't know how to execute. Your job as a leader is to go figure out how to get them all executing. You've got to start getting that drum roll going—that cadence—every day. Once that starts, its amazing: all of a sudden, it just kind of mushrooms up and you have a team that is focused on executing and one that is really winning."

Joseph Lawler of CMGI warned, "Too often, I think we give assignments, and we tell people to do something, fill in this spreadsheet, do this analysis. And people don't really think about how it fits into a broader context. I find that we're always more effective if . . . we explain to people what we're trying to do—here's the reason I want the analysis, here's how it fits into a broader context. Here's what I'm trying to understand." Looking at the same thing from the other side, Lawler advises those who are doing the research or the analysis to think, Where does this fit in with everything else? "Once you do it, stand back and be ready for the question that a generalist is going to ask you, which is much broader than just the analysis that you did."

Bill Nuti of NCR warned of what he calls the "disease of initiative-itis." This, he said, happens when "if you are like me and like a lot of other CEOs, you tend to multitask at a rate and at a pace most human beings cannot." It was a remarkable observation: "Initiative-itis is [when] you have so many things that have become top priorities for you that create multiple initiatives in the company . . . but frankly there are just too many for the organization to digest, and rather than making progress against any initiative, you've watered down your ability to focus on a few that are really important and drive them to fruition before you move to the next. So the digestive system of a company and how many initiatives it can digest is, I think, a great responsibility [for] the CEO."

It was Rick Dreiling who, for me, neatly captured the relationship between strategy and execution and helped me appreciate this point more fully. "Strategy," he said, "is all about the ability to execute on a plan, defining where you want to go and then executing against it. I think the business world is filled with visions that never get executed. Everybody's got ideas, but it is that ability to take that idea and turn it into a strategic vision that people can understand and are willing to do, and do it on a constant basis, day in and day out. To me that's the glory idea."

Do go for glory. That's a big part of wanting to lead. But bear in mind that there will be times when you might have to kick the doorframe in frustration. Javier Gutiérrez, with his skill for labeling things, calls this "the loneliness of power." We cannot always achieve what we strive for. Gutiérrez is simple and philosophical about this: "As human beings, we do not get things the way we want [them to be]." Much of this, he said, is associated with another of the frustrations of leadership—the absence of "total alignment"—everyone understanding the same message, striving for the same goal. This doesn't always happen, "and that is why the challenge of communicating in a good manner is essential," concluded Gutiérrez.

Don't Let Up

Once you get that cadence going, it's also up to the CEO to keep it up, never waver, and strive to be even better. One thing many of the CEOs I spoke to stressed was the importance of always improving. "Fidelity's been so successful that the danger is you become complacent," Bob Reynolds said. "I was really worried about that because the company's done phenomenally. But what I try to do is lay out much bigger goals. We're going to double by the end of this century. It took us sixty years to get to $1 trillion under management. We're going to be $2 trillion in five years. So everyone understood that we're still a growth company." His job, as he put it, was to "rally around to make sure everyone understood how big [the issue of] retirement was for the firm, and that it's going to be huge. It's the biggest opportunity in our business lives—the aging and the baby boomers."

Of course, part of rallying and getting the troops excited is building in bonus plans. "We started an innovation challenge where I put aside $10 million, and I said, 'We're going to reward good ideas,'" Reynolds said. "Some senior business leader said, 'All my people come up with good ideas already.' Forget it. We're going to do it." There's a fine line between complacency and celebrating success, and Reynolds doesn't agree with people who eschew the cheering. "I think you should enjoy it. It's exciting," he said. "If you're successful it should be fun, not a pain in the ass. This should feel great, because we've accomplished what we've set out to do." But for Reynolds, success should be followed immediately by the question, "Now, what's the next goal?" not, "Well, we hit this goal, we're done for the rest of our career."

Raimundo Morales of Banco de Crédito echoed this view: "When you are successful . . . do not wait for the problems before you change."

So keep moving. As Rick Dreiling explained, "In the private equity world or the public world, you are as good as your last quarter. And the frustrations are when you deal with human beings there is a curve there to get them where you need to get to. . . . I am a believer that success is a lousy teacher and the more successful you tend to be, the more behind you can get. . . ." I asked him to say why he thought success a lousy teacher. He said that success breeds complacency, and you begin to expect good things to come your way. If you are not careful, you stop learning and forget to push yourself and the organization forward.

Steve Shindler felt much the same way: "Our corporate culture is to be proud but never satisfied. What I mean by that is I want people coming into work every single day feeling good about what they did yesterday, last month, last quarter, last year. The results are strong and I'm proud of those results, and we're proud of you for producing those results. But 'never satisfied' means that we recognize that that's all rearview mirror stuff. What we've got in front of us is a steep hill to climb. It's an opportunity so we want to go after it because if we climb it, the business is going to be worth that much more."

Shindler was just being realistic. There are always going to be difficult things to navigate as you go on. "There's a lot of nasty, winding curves in that road as you go up the hill that they have to navigate through, but even though we've done well everything can still be improved," he said. "That's the definition of success: continuous improvement. You have to have both: the pat on the back, and have people feel good about it. But that is a momentary time of brief celebration and a recognition immediately of 'Okay, how are we going to build on that?' "

There is, therefore, a harder edge to the job than sometimes we allow ourselves to dwell on. Not too much patting oneself on the back allowed, not even too much applause for the team. There's work to be done. When I spoke to Walt Bettinger of Charles Schwab, he made this point at the end of our interview: "We talked a lot about the softer side . . . [but] . . . none of that means softness in terms of [being] soft around tough decisions, in doing what you need to do. In fact, if anything, I think they actually go together because you can't honor and serve the people you work for without the willingness to make tough decisions. You can't honor and serve the shareholders and the clients and employees without facing the fact that everybody around the leaders has accountability and responsibility and those who don't uphold their end of the bargain have to be removed. So I always make sure I talk with folks, that none of this means softness in terms of your willingness and ability to make tough calls."

And then there is the hard work. Sure, you'll take some time here and there for a proper break and to stay a human being, but you will have to keep looking and planning ahead. The circumstances of one of my interviews reminded me of this. I saw Kenneth Hicks at JCPenney headquarters in Plano, Texas, after Thanksgiving and before Christmas, so the whole headquarters was decorated and getting ready for Christmas. I assumed they had just gotten ready for the holiday season, but he said, "That was done three months ago. Now we're ready for Valentine's Day."

In the End, There's Only You Left to Blame

When the call goes out for those responsible, there's only one person in line, and that's you. On occasion that might appeal to your sense of honor—you were always taught to be the final frontier, the one who got the congratulatory calls for a job well done but also the one who was blamed for one done poorly. But on many, perhaps even most occasions it's about something less conspicuous and a lot more mundane: the dirty work. Goh Sik Ngee, who spoke so eloquently about the great responsibility he felt to so many people, also spoke of an unavoidable aspect of the job: downsizing. "[It's difficult] when you start dealing with the lower-level people whose income is not a lot, they don't have a lot of opportunity, and very often they are probably the sole breadwinner," Goh said. "And when you present

things—retrenching, for example—it doesn't affect me personally."
He recognized that it is part of the emotional struggle you have to go
through. "Nobody else in the company except you goes through that
struggle," he said. "The rest just follow your instruction, so emotionally, they don't feel guilty. The HR people dishing out the pink enve-
lope [say], 'I'm carrying out my duty as instructed by whomever.' But
I'm the person who says, 'Do it.' Sometimes it's quite emotional, and
nobody else in that company will share it with you."

John Kealey embraced the responsibility that comes with the job,
but warned that it cannot be taken lightly—it's one thing to say, this
is my decision, I stand by it, but it's another to be sure whether it was
the correct one. "I'm not complaining; I love the position, but you
have to be right. That's the reality of the CEO and the risks you take,"
he said. "You also have to accept that if the company is incredibly
successful it's because the team did a great job, and if it fails it's because the CEO didn't do a good job, period. You own that, you know
if it fails, first and foremost, you have failed because you own responsibility for the team."

Indeed, Steve Shindler said almost the same thing. "When office
decisions come up, even with all the input and benefit of how close
you are with your team, you're really alone. At the end of the day,
those toughest calls, they're on your shoulders. You're the one, you
get all the input you want, you try to feel as comfortable as you can,
but you've got to be comfortable enough to make that call. There's
no one standing side by side with you, sharing that responsibility or
accountability. I don't have anyone to turn to and ask, 'Should I do
this?' I can ask those questions, but the bottom line is, it's myself."

It seemed that for Rick Dreiling, it was responsibility tinged with
wonder: "No matter how hard you prepare yourself for that, or no
matter how good you think you are, it's a very interesting feeling that

first Friday when you go home and you suddenly realize, you know, this place is going to make it or not based on the decisions I make. And that is a pretty awesome feeling."

This acknowledgment that in the end it's down to you arose in my interview with Brian Sullivan. In fact, it was in the context of the frustrations that executives feel in the job, and he faced it head on: "I don't want to embrace the cliché, but the 'alone' factor is pretty significant. The CEO is and should be the only one thinking about certain things twenty-four/seven because the C-suite executives are fixed on their part of the business. CEOs should not take too much of the top people's time, therefore you have to find ideas elsewhere. That can be draining, but it simply goes with the territory. As far as overcoming these frustrations, that's the job, get over it."

Executive Summary

Broaden your shoulders. This job carries a tremendous amount of responsibility, not only for you, but for your shareholders, customers, employees, their families and their livelihood—and society at large. You'll be reminded of this every day.

If they are paying for your product, they're the ones who are right. The most important task for the CEO is to remember that customer service is a priority, no matter what industry you're in or where you're located. It's about how much value you can add and what you can provide for your customer, who is always first.

You set the tone and run the show. You are responsible for establishing and spreading a corporate culture that will help achieve your business goals and create the work environment that will help your employees feel valued. Be prepared to champion a corporate ethic and live and breathe it from the moment you walk into the office every morning—your employees look up to you and will follow your lead.

Make sure the work is done. One thing that sets leaders apart from everyone else is the ability to execute—you're the conductor who keeps the momentum going, even if you are not sure you're doing the right thing. You're bound to make mistakes, but it's important to learn to make unambiguous decisions based on the information you can gather quickly and efficiently.

No one told me there would be days like this. There are times when circumstances beyond your control conspire to undermine all your efforts. Financial and economic crises can pull the rug out from under your feet. You cannot prepare for such things, but you can dig deep down inside and find the strength to fight another day.

You're the one. The old cliché "the buck stops here" will sound like a familiar friend as you discover that when it comes down to it, there's no one to turn to and ask: Should I do this? But that's the job, so embrace the responsibility that comes with it.

Chapter 10

Why It's All Worth It in the End

We know by now that being part of the elite C-suite is demanding and difficult, and that getting there can be even harder. But it is clear to all of us who have either been there, seen people get there, or want to get there ourselves that the rewards are considerable. Yet that's something that perhaps we don't hear enough about. So I asked the executives I spoke to what they love about the job, what made the difficult climb to the top prove worthwhile.

I was struck by the fact that one of the first things many told me was that it was not necessarily their personal success that was most gratifying, but seeing the success of others—the satisfaction of seeing their employees do well and get ahead, and the fact that they have the ability to have a big impact on people's lives and career development. When they said these things, it was clear to me that they were not just making an empty statement but one they really meant. "If you're the type of person, and I think I am," John Swainson of CA, Inc. said, "who enjoys seeing people become capable, and that capability translating into them becoming more efficient and effective in their roles, and that effectiveness translating into a better company,

I think that's one of the great gratifications of this role. It's seeing how people can ultimately make the difference in organizations. And I won't say that I didn't understand that, at least at some level, but there's a lot about doing these jobs that you may understand at an intellectual level. It's quite different to actually experience it, and I would say that that's a profound difference."

John Kealey of iDirect went a step further and related it to his employees' personal success and prosperity. "iDirect was very successful and the employees benefited from it, so we allowed everybody to participate in the equity of the firm," he said. "It's the gratification outside of the workplace that makes me feel good, when people pull me aside and tell me about how they've built a college fund for the kids, and their wife quit work. I have a lot of people come up to me and tell me how much better their overall life is. We increased the workforce sixfold, most of them were professionals and were the primary source of income for those households. It's great because we've got a lot more families depending on the company, which is a lot of pressure, but there's also a lot of gratitude in that way."

Sanjiv Ahuja of Orange felt the same way, not only about his employees but about everyone else affected by the company's performance. "You realize you have three stakeholders that you work for—customers, shareholders, and employees. It gives you a sense of accomplishment when you see happy employees, when you see customers who are delighted, and shareholders who feel like they are being rewarded. That's what we're all about. We are the custodians of the shareholders."

Even when people leave the company and move on to new things, it is gratifying to Bob Reynolds of Fidelity. "I think you have a lot of pride in the people who work for you, to see them grow and expand. Some of the greatest pride today is seeing some of the old team move on and do other big things," he said. "As you're going through the process you don't totally realize what you're accomplishing because you're just trying to get after it day after day after day. In hindsight, when you have a chance to reflect, like when I made the decision to step down, it suddenly hits you. You're getting e-mails and letters from people about how you affected their lives and how being part of something that turned out great was something they'll never forget."

The more we talked about these things, the more I realized that the rewards of being at the head of a company also include the legacy you create and the satisfactions you feel when working with a successful team. Here are some of the things that, once you get to the top, you'll find rewarding—some obvious, some surprising—and worth the entire journey.

A Sense of Accomplishment

For Steve Shindler, it is that sense of everything falling into place. "It's gratifying when you can truly align those things that you think are important, and pull on all the right levers and step back at the end of each day and say, 'I think I'm hitting on all the right things,' and then to see the benefit from it," he said. Shindler experienced this on a grand scale, as mentioned in chapter 9, after seeing Nextel through a restructuring before it became NII Holdings. "Five years ago we were going through a restructuring process and had our backs against the wall. We started with a basic set of principles and said, 'We're going to go with disciplined focus on profitable subscriber growth, and look at metrics first.' Not like the land-grab scenario where everyone else was going to get as many customers as they could and end up losing half of them in a short period of time, because they weren't the right ones for their business. We kept those things in proper perspective, maintaining an entrepreneurial spirit in the culture right from the beginning, and recognized that we wanted to avoid the pitfalls of becoming a bureaucratic organization. We melded that in such a way that the surprise has been we were able to put that into a direction and a set of results that enabled us to go from $50 million in value to $14 billion in four years. It's all of the little things and how you work behind the scenes to get everybody into alignment that is exponentially powerful."

Rick Dreiling of Duane Reade told me he believes in "merciless devotion to execution," so one of the best parts of the job is seeing the results. "It's gratifying to be able to go out into the stores or manufacturing plants and see your strategic ideas being executed," he said. "When that happens, you know there's more. Results follow execution." Dreiling also stressed the rewards of working with those in private equity. "What is satisfying dealing with the private equity world is how supportive they are about articulating your plan. As long as you're marching to that tune, they're there for you and you don't have to deal with the stockholder. Finance people are very business savvy and focused. They know Rome wasn't built in a day. If it was a straight line to the top they wouldn't be paying what they pay for guys like us to do this stuff. And they are very, very supportive on the ups and downs."

Joseph Lawler of CMGI also finds tremendous reward in seeing something from start to finish, and how he affected it. "Maybe the greatest reward for me so far is having built a strategy, executing it, and seeing it come together," he said. "Seeing how the board fits into that, and how the management team, clients, and internal team fits into that is tremendously satisfying. This is the first time in a long time that the whole thing—and all the pieces—have come together."

Bill Nuti of NCR talked of the impact the job has on you, on your organization, and on people. "For us, when I first started here, we had thirty thousand employees, and those thirty thousand employees had families, and the impact you can have positively on not just your employees, but their families, was something that was not anticipated but greatly appreciated."

In the End, It's Your Decision That Counts

As much as you have to answer to everyone as CEO, you are at the same time making big decisions. "The most gratifying [aspect] for people who've worked in corporations before is that you have at least nominally more control than you've ever had before," Carl Bass of Autodesk said. "I say 'nominally' because you need to use your authority sparingly. But once your company is any significant size, your ability to know what's going on in all parts at all times or control all the activities is obviously limited. From appearance you can control everything but in reality you can't. Organizations have a little bit of a life of their own, but at least the gratification is that you do get to control a lot more than you ever had before, and you can affect the direction."

Bill Amelio of Lenovo also said he liked being able to influence things in a significant way. "You have the opportunity to craft a strategy, to put together a world-class team and essentially execute the way you see fit," he said. "If you ask my direct reports, they would tell you that I'm involved a lot in reviewing their execution."

Martin Homlish of SAP finds that he's also able to make real changes, in his case from a marketing perspective. "I really had the opportunity to make a difference in changing, frankly, the perception and then hopefully as part of changing the perception, changing the reality of the positioning of the company. In the marketing world, we're all about converting perception into reality and leveraging insight to provide foresight, and leveraging foresight to provide competitive advantage. So when you're sitting in the role as the top marketer and sitting in that C-suite corner office, you have both the opportunity and, frankly, the profound responsibility of driving—and in this case for SAP the initial requirements that I was given [were] to help change the position of the brand and the position of the company in the marketplace with all of the constituents—everything from employees all the way through influencers.

"Being given that responsibility is a very, very serious requirement, but being able to deliver on the responsibility is quite meaningful. It helps you understand what kind of an impact a single individual can have over the direction, and ultimately the impact you can have on changing the future of a company."

Of course, Homlish acknowledged that there are trade-offs (see chapter 9): "If you're aspiring to the corner office, it really is a very, very powerful feeling to know that you—one single individual—can truly make a difference. But it's also sobering to know that you have that much responsibility and influence. Not just this 'corporate identity,' but that much influence on many, many human beings relying on you to make the right decision and to use the right judgment. I expected it but it's quite different when you live it."

Constant Challenge

When you're at the top, you won't be looking for things to occupy your mind. Ron Williams of Aetna relishes how the job is a mental workout. "For me the intellectual challenge has always been something I've enjoyed," said. "The variety and complexity of problems that arrive at your desk tend to be intellectually stimulating, and often require more subtle solutions. If it was an obvious solution, it would have been solved somewhere else in the organization. I've always found that to be energizing—the fact that you sometimes face importantly unarticulated problems or solutions that need to be developed."

Likewise, Sanjiv Ahuja, who sees crises as opportunities, finds that his experience in turning around problems was the most rewarding. "If I look at my career, I've usually done turnarounds and taken businesses in a challenging position that either to the incumbents or others might have appeared as risky. Almost every time I've done that, [it's been] very satisfying and gratifying . . . both personally and professionally."

Walt Bettinger of Charles Schwab found that some of the toughest decisions and situations were the most rewarding as well. "You can't honor and serve the shareholders and the clients and employees without facing the fact that everybody around the leaders has accountability and responsibility. Those who don't uphold their end of the bargain have to be removed. Some of the most rewarding experiences, as difficult as they were, were talking with very senior executives who I had to let go. Sometimes they did nothing wrong; we just had too many of them. And they said to me, 'This conversation from some people would have been very difficult and I would have been very bitter. And having this conversation with you makes it okay. I understand.'"

Some CEOs simply thrive on the adrenaline and excitement of excelling, which is the case with François Barrault of BT Global services. "I like competition. I like goals. I like milestones," he said in his inimitable no-holds-barred style. "It is a structure I like and it also helps people to create a project together. That's something which I found very stimulating. In our world, every day is a new world. I am obsessed by competition. In this business you need to understand that everything is on the move, so there is what I call the winning differential, which is not a static value. So what is true today might be wrong in six months. I spent all my life, since I started working, to anticipate what the next model, what the next competition is. As soon as I execute the plan I already, in my mind, am in the next plan. It's a moving target."

Barrault sees that competition on various levels, not just in business performance, but in reaching out to people on a human level. "I have more tools to build something big, which is good for the community, the people, and the customers," he said. "I will never be a trader or an investment banker. I need to do something that brings things for the community. When you bring broadband to India or Africa, or when you help the company to learn some new services, I think it is fantastic." For Barrault this instinct is almost innate, and through his position he has the satisfaction of doing what he does best: working for the customer. "I have always had internal behavior that whatever I do, I need to bring something to others, and I've always been focused on what value I bring. It's a service, a product."

Seeing Your Employees Grow

A theme that came up repeatedly was the appreciation of working with employees and seeing them reach their potential. "I think the biggest gratification is watching people grow and develop," Ken Hicks of JC Penney said. "You see a person who was in one job and they move up a couple of levels, and you look at how they've grown professionally, what they're able to do, their responsibility and how they handle situations. There are people who you can look at and you see how they've matured over time." Now, said Hicks, "I'm reaching the point where I think everybody's a kid." But he has moments when he sees people he once thought of as young managing a difficult situation. "You know it's going to happen, but it's always great to see it because with so many people you say, 'I hope people grow and develop,' but when you watch it from day to day you don't see it change. You don't notice until you get to a situation and you see, 'Wow! That person has really developed and matured.'"

Different Corporate Cultures

Lucas Chow of MediaCorp said he came to appreciate the distinct cultures of companies he's worked for, experiences that were enhanced by his influential positions at all three—Hewlett-Packard, SingTel, and MediaCorp. The first experience he related was not as a CEO, but as someone who worked for twenty years at Hewlett-Packard. "Being Asian, you're full of respect, and I remember when I met the founder [I thought], 'Wow, this guy's a billionaire,' and so you have a lot of expectations because he's the founder of such a big company. So I tried to be polite and do the Asian thing. At that time he was already quite an old man. And I'm much younger than him, so I offered to carry his bag. He said, 'I'm fine, you don't have to.' Hewlett-Packard is very down-to-earth and people-oriented, which is something that from the Asian perspective I didn't expect, that my boss—a billionaire, guru, icon—would be so humble."

When Chow joined SingTel, it was a different story. "People called each other by 'Mister' and were very formal. I joined the company as a group director, then after that I was a VP, and so on. And even as a group director of the company, there is a lot of respect, and people look at you like 'Wow, you're the boss.' It was a very big contrast to HP, which is a very informal culture with everybody on a first-name basis. Now at MediaCorp, when I first entered the company the kind of respect they have for the top man is tremendous. When I walked into the canteen it created a stir, because apparently most CEOs hadn't walked into the canteen for a very long time. The moment I sat down the store owners and everybody ran over and asked, 'What can we do for you?' Within thirty minutes the whole company knew the CEO was in the canteen, but I was just there for a cup of coffee. That goes to show that different companies have different benchmarks and surprises."

Of course, the size, industry, and scope of a company have an effect on the kind of experiences you'll have, and Joseph Lawler reflected on the variety in his career trajectory now that he's in the top spot. "I started out at the Gillette company a hundred years ago," he said. "They moved me about every five or six months, which at the time felt just about right but it wasn't long enough for me to actually have stuck through a couple of cycles. When I reflect back on it I like to actually see people in responsibility for a couple of cycles. But they moved me very quickly. And it opened my mind to sales and marketing and finance and how some of those things work together."

Lawler then checked off the different types of companies he had worked for—an illustrious career summed up in a few sentences. But the effect is that he can now look back on a rich and rewarding experience. "I've been in a variety of different industries—retail, women's fashion, hunting, camping. I worked with a designer, I've had my own business. I've done a lot of varied things."

Privilege

Then of course there are the opportunities that being a CEO provides. "I enjoy the privileges it gives me and the doors it opens," Nadia Zaal of Al Barari said. "I have people contacting me all the time, and I meet really interesting people—people are what fascinate me more than anything else."

For CEOs one of the great privileges is to work with other great CEOs on their way up. Bill Amelio worked with Sam Palmisano of IBM and Larry Bossidy of AlliedSignal (who became chairman of Honeywell when the companies merged). "I had the opportunity to work with Sam Palmisano and learned some great techniques from him," Amelio said. "Sam taught me the power of putting an edge on things to ensure the team understands what is important and where a sense of urgency is required. Larry Bossidy was probably the single best coach that I worked for, because he took me under his wing. He was honest and direct. He had the courage to tell me when I was doing something wrong or headed down the wrong path. He knew. He didn't mince words. [He'd say], 'Hey, here's why I think you're going off the charts. You have to work on this, this, this, and this.' We had a great relationship." As you rise through the ranks, your opportunities to work with legendary CEOs will open up, too.

Raimundo Morales of Banco de Crédito named "recognition from people" and "respect" as two of the things that made him feel good about his job. But that was because those two things allow him to influence people, to be an opinion leader. "I guess it comes with your own personality, but also the title helps you a little bit, especially here in Latin America. People listen more to somebody who has a CEO title than somebody who doesn't have one."

Javier Gutiérrez of Ecopetrol also spoke of what he called "recognition received from people." It ranked alongside the other reward he said he felt in the job: the genuine gratitude of people in the company "even at the lowest level."

Teamwork

Rick Dreiling said one of the most rewarding aspects of being a CEO is watching his employees grow, and, specifically, he values the experience of putting together a strong team. "The true gratification for me has been assembling the team that I have and watching them produce," he said. "It's the people who get down here and roll up their sleeves and put the strategies around those ideas. That is tremendously gratifying. And the one, too, that I think most CEOs would tell you is that when people understand it, there is no limit to what they can do because they get it. The light goes on and sometimes you feel like a college professor who just taught someone how to multiply four times four, and they say 'Sixteen!' And you get so excited."

Dreiling also makes a point to learn with his employees, and will keep up on the latest and go over it with his team. "I'll circulate articles and once a month we'll sit down and just talk about them—trends, management techniques. [We talk about] companies that are doing incredibly well and why they are doing so well, and should we be more like GE or more like these guys. I view part of my responsibility to grow [my employees] into their jobs. And it's very gratifying when you see these things happening. Because if they're doing their jobs, they're saying, 'That was really a great meeting. I'm going to do the same thing with my vice presidents.'"

Terrance Marks of Coca-Cola also enjoys the teamwork: "One of the most fulfilling aspects is the ability to pull together a team and help it function on a high level, and really facilitate the development of teamwork," he said. "We've been involved in a significant amount of change and work. We're changing everything about our business. You've got your core team, extended team, which includes the senior leadership, and our business units that are scattered throughout

North America. And pulling them in and benefiting from their input to the formulation of strategy has been very powerful. You know
all along that if people haven't inputted into a process, they weren't
likely to have ownership. That's pretty fundamental, but it's even
more powerful than I think I realized coming into it."

Joseph Lawler not only has pride in leading a strong team, but
also learns a great deal from his team, and considers that to be one
of the many rewards of the C-suite. "I've learned a lot about how to
lead, manage, and work with a group of individuals who are very
smart. Several of them have done what I've done, sometimes on a
much greater scale, sometimes a much smaller scale, with very different perspectives," he said.

Molding People's Futures

Walt Bettinger finds immense satisfaction in his interpersonal relationships, not only with employees but with clients. "I think one of
the most gratifying aspects over the years is seeing people who
came into the business, had a client focus, and attained success beyond what they aspired to," he said. "Seeing others in situations of
accomplishment or achievement has certainly been inspirational to
me. Another inspirational thing to me is getting to know clients and
[see them] achieve their dreams. I get regular letters from people
who will share their stories: 'I became a Schwab client twenty-five
years ago and I had this, and you helped me along the way and now
I have this.' Or 'I've been able to do this,' or achieve this dream,
fund this charitable effort, care for a parent. One of the real bless-
ings I've experienced over the years working in financial services is
[being part of] an industry that can change people's lives for the
better."

Bettinger said Schwab's first president, Larry Stupski, was fond of saying, "We're not in the business of making neckties. This is people's financial future." "That very simple saying is something I've always tried to remember. I think what he meant is that, without trying to denigrate the business of making neckties, the necktie someone wears is not likely to change their lives, and we do. We have a responsibility, whether it was back in the days of building a retirement services business, making sure people got their fair and just pensions, that they were funded properly, that companies acted responsibly in the funding, into the years of working in Schwab and in the retail side. This is about more than that. This is about having a positive impact on people's lives."

Bill Swanson of Raytheon told me a story that brought together many aspects that have come up in this book, from networking to recruiting. It was a by-product of the constant outreach and connecting he does in his daily life. On a trip to Pebble Beach, he and his wife stayed at an inn where, in true Bill Swanson fashion, he struck up a conversation with the young man working at the reservations desk. He discovered that the man was a graduate student at Stanford working at the inn for the summer. He was a mechanical engineer, and Swanson asked if he had a job. He didn't, so Swanson said, "I work for a company and we've got forty thousand engineers. Do you want to stay in California? We have a huge operation down in El Segundo." Swanson gave him his card, and the following June the man graduated and called Swanson, who hired him.

"He was a very smart young man and went to work in El Segundo. He met a nice young woman and within a year he was married. He sent me one of the nicest notes of how a serendipitous meeting had changed his entire life, and that he's met the woman of his dreams. She works there, and we call them 'Ray Rays,' which is what we call a husband and wife working for the company, because both work for

Raytheon. Here's this couple who have a very bright future. And you look at it and say, 'You've had an impact.' "

Indeed, Swanson has touched many people, and he's known for it. One of his employees says that often when she gets on a plane and chats with the person next to her, when they ask where she works, they say, "Do you know Bill Swanson?" and then tell a story about meeting him at a dinner or other event. And many of those meetings result in a serendipitous connection that adds to a CEO's legacy.

In the end, that's what it's all about—your legacy. Michael Dell has a view of the intersection of business and society that is both unique and powerful: "Ensuring we have resources for growth means much more than ensuring component supply. It also means attracting the best possible talent, ensuring we're protecting the environment, and partnering with suppliers and customers to make impactful changes from workplace policies to emissions reductions. A good example of this is Dell's engagement in the fight against HIV. HIV affects our employees, customers, suppliers, and communities worldwide, and ultimately, our business. We took our HIV prevention efforts even further this year by joining the RED campaign. This offers our customers some of our very best products, and at the same time helps fight AIDS in Africa."

As a CEO, you will have the opportunity to affect countless lives, some of whom you will never even know. This is an awesome responsibility, one that cannot be borne by everyone. Beyond everything that you will deal with in the corner office, this is the one responsibility that, if carried out well and honorably, will live long after you have vacated the C-suite. It is a unique opportunity, one that is bigger than you and the company. The successful CEOs I've met all over the world take this responsibility seriously. If you want to get to the C-suite and leave your mark there, you should, too.

Executive Summary

You will get results. Yes, you answer to a great number of people, but that's not the same thing as them telling you what to do. A place in the corner office affords you real influence and power and the opportunity to think, plan, and execute on a scale and with responsibility that few other jobs get close to.

Your employees grow with you. Many CEOs spoke about their role with a parental pride, and you'll be rewarded by seeing employees grow and respond to challenges and rise to the occasion as they progress through their careers. And there is little that is more fulfilling than picking and leading an enthusiastic team.

You have permanent access to the VIP pavilion. Many doors will open to you, filling your days with interesting and influential people who will find you interesting and influential in return. You will learn about and visit other countries, cultures, and companies. And so your mind will be stimulated daily by new things, by challenges and by ideas.

And it's personal. You will have the power to change the lives of individuals and large groups of individuals, and not only will this very responsibility sometimes take your breath away, but when you see what you can do, you will feel it deeply. Sometimes you will know the names of the people whose lives you touch; sometimes there will be too many for that; but often what it does to you will be almost spiritual.

Afterword

by Brian Sullivan

No one becomes a leader the day they become a CEO. Indeed, true leaders influence people throughout the course of their careers. As explained in this book, there are many different paths to the top, but the consistent personality traits of honesty, integrity, good communication, self-confidence, and tenacity are the core criteria for leaders. The men and women who run companies today started honing their skills from day one of their careers and continued developing them regardless of how they got to the top.

That being said, what leadership lessons have we learned from Umesh's book? For me, it felt like I had private meetings with today's top CEOs, complete with their fresh, honest insights about their own personal career trajectories. Umesh met with leaders from around the world at companies across the spectrum, and while he let the experts do the talking, he distilled for us the most valuable bits of information, knowing what would be most useful for young managers—resulting in this invaluable insider's guide for executives.

I'll take just a moment to add that Umesh couldn't be better suited to bring you the insights in this book. He has been involved with executive search since the nineties, and, in fact, was a key player on the team that brought me to CTPartners in 2004. I immediately gravitated toward him because of his global insight, his unique assessment skills, and his desire to find the best person for the job. He knows what it's like on the other side too, having previously held the positions of COO of R&R International and president of R&R Global, an off-shore engineering company—well before "off-shoring" was part of the lexicon. He was a successful operating executive that made the transition from being a leader of a global company to a senior executive in a global operation.

Umesh brought his unique world view to the table as he put together the inspiring roster of CEOs for this book, calling upon his broad network. He spent hours on planes to meet executives around the world, something that is hardly unfamiliar to him. In fact, I like to call him a "global citizen" for whom globe-trotting, as it were, is old hat. He was born in India but educated in the United States and settled in the heart of the Midwest. His cross-cultural know-how enables him to guide CEOs in their assessments of both executives who are based in the U.S. and those who have extensive overseas experience.

Indeed, Umesh is as comfortable in New York City as he is in London, Singapore, or Mumbai. For this book, one day he would be en route to meet Lucas Chow in Singapore to hear how Chow got to the top spot at Mediacorp. On another day he was back with his family in Ohio, where he met his neighbor, Walt Bettinger, the COO and likely future CEO of Charles Schwab. And then he went back East to Bangalore, India, to meet with Kiran Mazumdar of Biocon and pick her brain on the ins and outs of running a major technology company.

In his research, Umesh found exactly the right people to address the challenges for the up and coming CEO. Bill Swanson of Raytheon, for example, exemplifies the importance of communicating. Umesh drew anecdotes from Swanson that illustrate how people are motivated by wanting to work for someone who believes that they are as important as the product being manufactured. It's very clear that leadership is about communication, listening, and having a consistent message in good times and bad (we saw this, too, when Steve Shindler of Nii Holdings described to Umesh what it was like to stand in front of his team when faced with bankruptcy in 2001). Both CEOs demonstrate the metaphor of how water flows downhill in a company. It's important to foster great communication—which will result in greater success and common goals.

In another example of developing employee relations, Kiran Mazumdar spoke to Umesh of her unusual habit, at least in the more traditional India, of eating in the company cafeteria and insisting her employees call her by her first name. The confidence in one's leadership to break tradition in how senior executives interact with people at all levels on the team has enabled Mazumdar to break through the glass wall as well as the glass ceiling to create a high performance culture.

On that note, Mazumdar gave valuable insight about working as a woman in a corporate culture dominated by men. Nadia Zaal of the Dubai real estate development corporation Al Barari had similar challenges. Zaal ran against the norm on two levels: there aren't many women in real estate in the world, much less in Dubai. She shows that individual leadership is paramount to strategy.

It's not just a coincidence that Umesh's dream team of CEOs is an international one that can reflect on the very real challenge of globalization. In the fifties and sixties, CEOs felt that applying their culture as well as their expertise was a way to enter new markets. Today's successful CEO realizes that embracing local market customs and conditions is essential in being able to influence change in an organization. The global CEO lives in the country, eats the food, and breathes the air of his constituents and customers.

The executive voices in this book also lend insight to career trajectories that aren't limited to a single industry or duty. Umesh tracked down Todd Stitzer of Cadbury Schweppes who worked in law and marketing before arriving at the global giant. Careers often span multiple industries; however, the cornerstones of leadership transcends specific industry expertise, which is exemplified by Stitzer. Whether someone's core competency lies in marketing, finance, or product development, it is a true leader who adapts to the needs of the organization at a particular point in time versus staying within their comfort zone regardless of its immediate need.

And while the world is moving faster and new technologies take over, Umesh took care to assemble leaders from all types of companies, from Terry Marks of Coca-Cola Enterprises to Nandan Nilekani of Infosys Technologies. Tech companies move at a mile a millisecond, but even legacy companies present their challenges—and up-and-coming managers need the insight from those inside the walls of a range of companies to get a full picture. It takes leadership, skill, and fortitude to take the dramatic steps needed to move a strong franchise to the next level. Companies need to be ambidextrous. The development of new products within an organization that dominates its sector requires fresh thinking from the CEO on one hand while the other hand continues to improve efficiency of the core product.

Ultimately, Umesh's book gives you access to the people behind some of today's most powerful companies. True leaders are happy to be forthcoming with their stories. While they are proud of their successes, they're willing to share their personal, good, bad, and ugly stories of how and why they got there. This kind of insight from such a broad array of successful leaders is an inspiration to any career-focused executive who needs to understand that success comes a step at a time, not as a bolt of lightning out of the air. Let this book guide you.

Acknowledgments

An endeavor of this magnitude cannot be embarked upon without a great deal of help. First, my sincere thanks to Brian Sullivan, the Chairman and CEO of CTPartners, for not only letting me spend time and effort on this book but backing it up with the support of the entire organization globally. I could not have started this without Jeffrey Krames from Portfolio, who first inspired, then cajoled, and eventually whipped me into shape to complete the manuscript. Many people helped me throughout the writing process and I thank all of them for their unwavering support and dedication—Jennifer Silver, Beth Kwon, Graham Watts, Mila Petty, Nawf Tannous, and all the associates of CTPartners. Special thanks to the partners of the firms around the world (Bob Forman, Buster Houchins, Chris Berger, Chris Conti, Daniel Soh, Debra Germaine, Grace Borrelli, Jamie Carter, Jim DiFillippo, Joe McCabe, Karin Brandes, Kathryn Yap, Maria Mejia, Marc Gasperino, Martin Noakes, and Ron Porter) that helped make the introductions to the C-suite residents for this book. Without their help, there would have been nothing to write about. Thanks to all the wonderful people at Penguin/Portfolio for their professional help as they patiently taught me the inner workings of the publishing industry. Many others provided the energy for me to enjoy the writing from scratch to finish. I thank them all. Finally, I could not have done this without the support of the women in my life: my wife, Anu; my mother, Sulochana; and my sister, Sapna, who provided continuous encouragement throughout the process.

Index